THE SECULAR GRAIL

THE SECULAR GRAIL

Christopher Dewdney

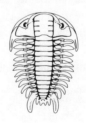

A Patrick Crean Book

Somerville House Publishing
Toronto

Canadian Cataloguing in Publication Data

Dewdney, Christopher, 1951-
The secular grail

ISBN 0-921051-96-4 (bound)   ISBN 0-921051-92-1 (pbk.)

I. Title.

PS8557.E846S42 1993   C818'.5407   C93-093456-3
PR9199.3.D48S42 1993

Design: Gordon Robertson
Cover Art: Andreas Zaretzki
Printed in Canada

A Patrick Crean Book

Published by Somerville House Publishing,
a division of Somerville House Books Limited,
3080 Yonge Street, Suite 5000, Toronto, Ontario M4N 3N1

Somerville House Publishing acknowledges the financial assistance of the Ontario Publishing Centre, the Ontario Arts Council and the Ontario Development Corporation.

The author wishes to thank Oliver Meurer for his technical assistance and Barbara Gowdy for her editorial advice.

CONTENTS

SLEIGHTS OF MIND

POWER DREAMS

GROUND OF THE IDEAL

SHADOWS OF THOUGHT

FOREWORD

The Secular Grail is a collection of essays, prose fragments and deliberations on a variety of topics. These include cities, technology, natural history, sexuality, the nature of consciousness, dreams and culture. There are also a number of meditations on language and writing.

For the most part the text consists of condensed, essentialized statements. There is little of literary or scholastic convention in them. Although the pieces are grouped according to subject they are also arranged in a series of modular units that do not have to be read in order.

The unstated premise of *The Secular Grail* is that the mind and body are one and that the heart and mind are also one. (The heart, the seat of the emotions, is physically located in the mind/brain.) It also holds that curiosity is innate to the human spirit—that it is a primal, emotional drive—and that science is the impartial engine of curiosity. Furthermore, it posits that there is no division between nature, culture and technology. Vinyl is as natural as lichen.

Our personality, our essence, who we are, is like a one-of-a-kind software that can run only on a single, unique computer. When this computer ends so does the software.

Although I am an agnostic, I believe that existence is miraculous and, for the most part, explicable. At the same time I also believe that, ultimately, all explanations derive from an indivisible mystery at the heart of existence.

THE SECULAR GRAIL

CITY
STATES

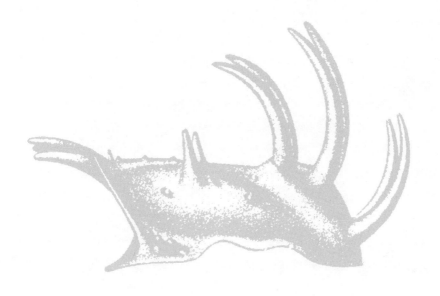

E

CHRONOPOLIS

*T*HE CITY is a time mosaic. It is a living archaeological aggregate of forgotten civilizations, of periods within decades, eras within centuries. The city is a simultaneous matrix of cultural empires, of invisible districts and regions. It is an infinitely graduated series of fashions and habits in which the individual is simply another arbitrary designation, a border that dissolves into the nested identities of the metropolitan psyche. Layers of prior styles, architectures and entertainments fade incrementally, one into the next, superimposed finally in the simultaneous levels of a protean urban vortex.

The city is spotted with islands, culs-de-sac of time where a previous decade, a prior century, stands untouched. A 1914 newspaper lying yellow on the floor of an attic cracked open for renovations. The heraldic limestone gates of the waterfront expressway. The tired hands of a middle-aged waitress, her movements a choreographed testament to an identity unchanged over thirty years, her make-up identical in the bathroom mirror each morning, a gestural fossil of forgotten fashion. The impassive stone faces at the summit of old bank towers, stoic trade deities of the early thirties staring into a future that has come and gone. Abandoned transfers from a night-bus lying in the early morning light.

Brazilian children run through the market crowds on a summer evening. Dusty sunlight through an old streetcar window on the first warm sunset in February, the streetlights flickering on, purple against the incandescent gold of the bank towers. The first breath of wind from an approaching subway train not yet audible or visible.

CITY STATES

A METROPOLIS is equivalent to a vehicle, and its citizens are all passengers moving through a financial landscape. Cities wax and wane within economic ecologies. They flourish according to their strategic location in the variable matrices of trade-routes and information-processing hierarchies. Cities are the only real distinct geopolitical entities within the urbanized Western industrial hemisphere.

Cities are fictional environments. They are ambient identities that, in terms of variety from one city to the next, have recognizable "looks" that their citizens wear as cosmetic name tags. Allegiance to city comes before allegiance to country. One's city is a familial membership.

The recent core renaissance is the result of the paradoxical desire for urbanization initiated by telecommunications and the personal computer. These devices originally exerted a decentralizing influence on the city. When offices no longer had to be centralized, and executives had the ability to telecommute without leaving their country homes, an immediate nostalgia for the urban environment arose. Once it had been technologically transcended by the professional classes, the city, and especially its downtown core, acquired a retro-cachet.

The city state is a telecommunications cocoon. The success of small, personal telecommunication devices hinges on their appeal as fashion accessories. Design is as important as function in the increasingly public arena of private communication.

4

RIOT COMMAND

A HIGH-END TENOR, preferably with a hysterical edge to
it, is the optimum frequency for command. Mid-range
frequencies are hard to distinguish from sirens, breaking glass
and ambient urban rumble.

Hyper-bass is an aural X-ray that penetrates the interiors of
buildings. As such it is an act of cultural aggression as much as it
signifies sexual availability.

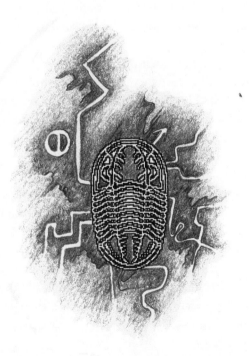

PSYCHOPOLIS

*T*HE GRID of the city is a control structure developed by urban planners to contain insurrection. Overcrowding creates higher hormonal activity in the individual. Self-assertion in aggressive public-transit environments leads to stressful levels of adrenaline. The constant violation of individual physical privacy, the result of competition for placement in line-ups, leads to muscle armouring and protective, ultimately bent, postures. Excitedness and adrenaline are a biologically enforced patriotism locking citizens into the high-population-density urban matrix.

The function of ambulances, of all sirened vehicles, in fact, is to inject adrenaline into circulation and maintain the "high" of background fear. The professional classes sustain this same high with news, an all-news station providing a constant low-key adrenaline rush, like an intravenous drip. This elevated vigilance, inherent in the diluted aggressive state of the ordinary city-dweller, is similar to the action of amphetamine. Security, which unlike health care is not subsidized by the government, has become an industry that entrenches paranoia and isolation.

The city is a vast corporate hormonal loop. Mass levels of gonadotropins are manipulated by erotic advertising. Elevated levels of endorphins in jogging executives anaesthetize their social conscience. Unbridled greed, along with the disappearance of the manufacturing sector, triggered the recession of the early nineties.

The mascot of the hormonal village is the psychopath—charming, witty, guiltless and deadly.

THE CODED CITY

$\mathcal{S}$YMBOLS confine attention to a single point. A traffic signal is a signifier, a unit of meaning in the urban environment. The entire city caters to a symbolic perceiver. Thus, something occupying a relatively small portion of the total visual field, like a traffic light, receives a disproportionate amount of attention because of its significatory function. Activated components (signs, lights, sounds) are nodal points of attention within a second-order environment. This second-order environment is the human cultural context, itself an intense socio-mythological field of interpretation.

The whole panorama of an urban setting can be "read." There are not only the obvious first-order linguistic referents—symbols, characters, letters and numbers—but also a profusion of extralinguistic signifiers (in the Barthean sense) in every surface and texture that meets the eye. Through format and typographical design this semi-opaque film of second-order signification even insinuates itself into first-order referents and is every bit as laden with nuance as the letters and numbers themselves. Identifying these second-order signifiers is a perceptual exercise in itself.

Take, for example, a typical bar interior, with stools, counter, cash register and beer coolers, etc. To begin with, colour-code all first-order signifiers (numbers and letters) a purple-blue (the magical hue of signification). Next, turn your attention to a commonplace object within the "bar" context—the cash register, say. With all its first-order signifiers colour-coded and demarcated, the majority of the register's surface is still unaccounted for. It is a fairly late-model register whose form, like most objects in this bar, is a trade-off between function and design. That is to say, its appearance is based on marketing notions of consumer trends in chassis formats, themselves in an uneasy relationship with utility. Because a cash register is a useful object its design can never impede its function, which remains basically unchanged through successive models. There is another general rule here as well: the higher the utilitarian charge, the lower the symbolic content.

It is difficult to free ourselves from perceiving our environment without the influence of the second-order signification we are habituated to. Wherever choice or taste have been supposedly exercised, it is important to see that these concepts are completely subjective, rarely straying outside of the subliminal hermeneutic realm. Consider the "tasteful" Italian-designed bar stools lined up along the counter. We assume that the trend towards "modern" simplicity is an evolutionary one, ridding furniture of useless ornamentation. In actuality we are just applying another system of aesthetic parameters. Our criteria have not transcended subjectivity; there is little difference between the criteria that drive "kitsch" designs and "tasteful" ones.

Let's examine an even less obvious example—the wood panelling used variously throughout the bar. Why was that particular shade of stain, on the cooler doors, chosen over innumerable other competing shades? Why that particular darkness for the bar hardwood? All of these available choices indicate a constantly changing matrix of fashion and trends, covert assumptions aimed at creating certain ambiences. These ambiences themselves suggest specific narratives—the "boy meets girl" narrative of the bar's retail myth, for instance. Such retail lures are made all the more precise by marketing studies.

Decoding second-order environments is one of the first steps towards extrication of the self.

CONTROL, OBSERVATION AND TRANSIT ANXIETY

*O*BSERVATION is subjectively perceived as a form of control. Take commuters waiting for a bus. By craning their necks and searching the distant traffic they feel that they hasten the bus's arrival. This activity pacifies their anxiety about the dilatory vehicle even though, logically, the bus will be neither hastened nor delayed by their watching and waiting. Furthermore, there is an anxiety attendant to the transition zone between waiting and moving, arising from being committed to transit while still being capable of self-propulsion. There is also the anticipatory anxiety of relinquishing self-control to a larger force, not to mention the uneasiness that comes from waiting for any event.

The tension of uncertainty is heightened even more by lack of visual confirmation. This is why airport terminals create low-key anxiety. The anticipated arrival or departure is blocked from view. Pacing and repetitive gestures—neurotic activities endemic to bus terminals, airports and train stations—attest to a temporal claustrophobia shared by all those caged in the unnatural demarcation between transit and stasis.

The greater the vista, the calmer are those who wait. In a large enough panorama, such as that afforded by a mountain in the centre of a plain, a vehicle can be tracked from such a great distance that it could be said to have arrived as soon as it is seen, even if a lot of time has to elapse before it is actually there. The vehicle's appearance in the visual field is a type of ontological representation, and tracking the vehicle is perceived as a form of control.

Once you have committed yourself to the role of passenger, your anxieties shift to concerns about lack of control over the handling of the moving vehicle. Certain passengers feel a strong need to communicate with the driver in order to contribute to the vehicle's control. In airplanes this need has to be sublimated entirely, hence the fear of flying. In automobiles, however, passengers have direct access to the driver and can allay their anxieties by delivering manoeuvring options.

HOSTAGES
OF CULTURE

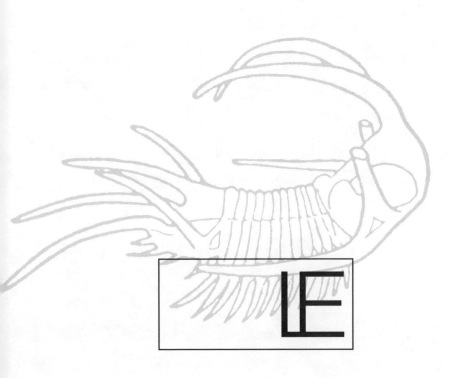

LE

TELEPHONE
TERRITORIALITY

---

*W*E ALL POSSESS a territory of personal privacy, an invisible social field surrounding us that is subconsciously acknowledged by others. This territory is flexible, diminishing in crowds and expanding in open spaces. During hostile or aggressive confrontations this boundary becomes critical; a transgression results in violence or retreat.

The telephone cuts across all territorial conventions during hostile or aggressive interactions. We are presented with a totally novel situation, evolutionarily speaking, when a discarnate stranger (the credit manager from a local telephone exchange, for example), not only trespasses personal territory but proceeds with overt verbal aggression past the point at which adrenaline levels would normally cause physical violence. The skilled aggressor can easily out-manoeuvre the helpless rage of his or her victim.

TELEPHONES
AND INTIMACY

---

*T*HE TELEPHONE is an intimate, though masked, personal telecommunications device. It is masked in the sense that by not seeing your conversational partner you can be both intimate and impersonal at once. This affords all the easy familiarity you feel with pets, whose affections are unqualified by judgements about your personal value or attractiveness. The theatrical nuances and capabilities of the discorporeal voice are liberated and heightened, at the same time facial and bodily expressions are invisible, focusing emotional energy on the voice alone.

AURAL SPACE

---

*T*HE CAR is an aural space, a glassed-in entertainment pod with a hypnotic, constantly changing visual panorama projected onto the windshield. This is why we like to listen to music in cars—the changing linearity of the passing landscape mirrors the temporal transformations of the music. The driver is mesmerized by the ever-expanding vanishing point. Auto-TV will continue to be a marginal component of automobile entertainment systems, whereas car stereos and cellular telephones will ultimately be ubiquitous.

POWER PHONING

---

*A*UTOMOBILES are devices for amplifying the unconscious. A car's responsiveness to will empowers the projective energy of the driver. This, in turn, acts hypnotically to
elicit his or her unconscious. Cars are disinhibitory, womb-like
environments that make drivers regress into an infantile state.
The deeper behaviour of traffic flow, though regulated by
imposed codes of order, is organized along unconscious lines.
Aggression is more overt. The instant you step into a car you
transform into your repressed persona. Witness the anger, the
petty competition, the risk-taking, the singing, the introspective
faces of nose-picking drivers.

The cellular telephone is the ultimate wedding of two very
private, tactile environments. The interior space of an automobile is an abbreviated, mobile living room. It is an internal den
insulated from the harsh realities of the outer world. This quality is heightened by the presence of a telephone. The nesting of a
cellular phone within the subconscious matrix of the car means
that you can now talk to your friends from the security of your
own unconscious mind. The telegenic power inherent in con-
versing with someone while immersed in such an intimate space
is irresistible.

FAX TO SHREDDER—
THE EVALUATION OF
NEW TECHNOLOGIES

---

*L*IKE the telephone answering machine, the fax is not really an invention, nor is it all that new. The technology has been in place for fifty years. Police departments have been using fax machines for over forty years. What has changed recently are the unit production cost variables that have made the technology more available. Looking at the history of telecommunications as a sequence of inventions, enhancements and demographic revolutions, we can evaluate any "new" technology that comes into play. The fax machine is simply the enhancement of the telephone, which, itself, was the enhancement of the telegraph. Fax machines have become popular because they are perceived as an empowering telecommunicative icon in the hierarchical environment of the hyper-materialist office of the nineties. Their function is incidental to their symbolic content—the secret, bourgeois thrill of actually faxing something.

ADVERTISING
AND PERCEPTION

*A*DVERTISING degrades perceptual confidence and accuracy by creating images that are causally naive. For example, a recent billboard ad tried to convey the idea that the reproduction quality of a brand of colour film was so lifelike that a photograph of a parrot (which was depicted in the billboard) would fool a house cat into clawing at it. The cat was shown at the moment just after it had ripped the photo of the parrot. A closer look at the "rip," however, revealed that it was a monstrosity, an idealized tear meant to look *more* like a rip than a natural rip.

Such visual hyperbole runs through all of our imagery in the cinema, television, magazines and the entire fabric of mass-consumer society. We are being subconsciously conditioned to accept a travesty of perception. Things have to be doctored to look more natural. People can no longer perceive naturality when they see it. This is an extension of the same invidious logic that trivializes the content of journalistic prose to cater to a hypothetical "common reader" who is condescendingly described as being unable to understand scientific concepts or terms that have more than two syllables.

Advertising habituates us to a visually symbolic code of interpretation by iconifying visual data. It does this to ensure the momentum of its transmission. Like the exaggeration utilized for projective purposes in theatre, advertising has developed a shorthand vocabulary of larger-than-life symbols. It is creating a synthetic inventory of drained images.

EXCLUSIVE
SURFACES

ASTE is an identifying characteristic, not altogether unrelated to disposable income and education, that divides the
carriage trade from the blue-collar retail zone. A few years ago a
watch company retailing an expensive gold watch displayed a
billboard ad consisting of a photograph of the watch lying on
wet, rough granite. The irregular natural surface is particularly
beloved to the carriage-trade class, signifying a romantic natural
order reminiscent of their summer retreats. Recently these
rough or deliberately antiqued surfaces have been enjoying a
renaissance amongst the rich, particularly in interior design.
Quasi-decayed natural surfaces are incomprehensible to the
blue-collar class, who spend a lot of time contriving to be
surrounded by clean, bright surfaces. The deliberately damaged
patina of the interior walls of luxury condominiums and
clothing stores, for example, is inaccessible to those who do not
have the luxury of appreciating the aesthetics of decay. The
blue-collar class can afford neither the rough surface nor the
exquisitely finished surface.

FAST FOOD

---

*F*AST FOOD is reverse lipo-suction in corporately designed environments.

ARTIFICIAL I
NTELLIGENC
E IS THE GRAI
L OF SECULAR
HUMANISM

THE MISAPPLICATION
OF DARWINISM

---

*T*HE THEORY of evolution has been culturally appropriated and misapplied in the mytho-economic realm of everyday life. This misapplication has resulted in enormous industrial and consumer waste, not to mention substandard goods and built-in obsolescence. The "survival of the fittest" mentality is the ultimate rationalization for cutthroat business practices and leveraged buyouts.

Inherent in our misapplied Darwinism is a latent racism towards "primitive" cultures, even though the cultural realm is almost completely outside the scope of evolution. At the same time, our relation to our own "primitive" human ancestors is skewed. "Cavemen" are portrayed in our media as functional retards instead of the highly evolved hominids they actually were.

MONOTHEISM
AS ANT TRAP

*C*HRISTIAN IDEOLOGY was the primary infection of the Roman Empire. As the Empire lay rotting its body was looted by successive waves of vandals who unwittingly carried the infection of Christianity back to their homelands in much the same manner that ants carry particles of Ant Trap into their nests. The virus proliferated like wildfire throughout northern Europe and within centuries mutated into several new forms.

Post-Hellenized Europe was ripe for the infection of Christianity, and existential fear became the main mode of transmission. Amongst culturally and technologically debased pagan peoples Christianity was an opportunistic conceptual system that allowed them to adapt to the social and technological upheavals that preceded it.

ATOMIC JEHOVAH

---

*O*NE of the most ancient concepts of Judaeo-Christian civilizations has finally materialized. Monotheistic, biblical power is now incarnate in the terrible destructiveness of nuclear weapons. Additionally, the notion of invisible agents of death, such as those that played such a sinister role in the original Passover, foreshadows radiation-sickness and biological weapons. The power of an omniscient, vengeful god who can decipher licence plates from space is now incarnate, and the seven plagues are housed in the war councils of the world nuclear powers.

The weaponry of the twentieth century is something we've been conceptually prepared for for thousands of years.

BIOLOGICALLY
DETERMINED
COMMUNITIES

---

*I*NTIMATE social circles that in the past were determined by common interests or economic milieu are being increasingly determined by sexually transmitted diseases. A glance at the personal listings in newspapers reveals much. Sexual compatibility is now based on matching sexually transmitted viruses in a sort of pathological membership. Ads placed by afflicted individuals describe which virus group they are a member of almost before any personal characteristics are listed. Furthermore, there are special clubs and organizations that cater to large numbers of viral monotypes. Established associations for herpes carriers include exclusive clubs and dating services, almost as if their members were privileged, their stigma transforming into the entrance card to a new social order. Organizations catering exclusively to members who test HIV-positive are now springing up.

You could go on to speculate that, in a subtle way, these groups might also be behaviour-specific. Although, presumably, they exhibit the usual spectrum of human diversity, there might also be an underlying consanguinity, as it were, a latent rapport, distilled and enhanced by the recognition that the organization confers. This common factor might be what brought them all together in the first place, what made them candidates for their mutual disease above and beyond the transmission necessities of a specific virus.

As we discover more and more low-grade conditions, particularly those outside the socially stigmatized sexually transmitted diseases (like chronic-fatigue syndrome and newly identified viral disorders) there will be more and more of this new social ordering. Eventually, not to be included in one of these organizations could make you feel left out.

ANYTHING W
ORTH KNOWI
NG YOU KNO
W ALREADY

THE TRIUMPH
OF ADOLESCENCE

A DOLESCENCE, for many Americans, is the most important period of their lives. Certainly it dominates their
entire culture, particularly music, film, television and sports.
Americans enter adolescence around the ages of nine to eleven
and leave it—fighting tooth and nail alongside their cosmetic
surgeons—somewhere between the ages of fifty and sixty. Then,
instead of entering a period of delayed maturity, they become
shrivelled adolescents, pathetic social outcasts afflicted with the
inexplicable disease of aging. Americans are the first people on
the planet to pass directly from adolescence to senility.

In America, not only has late childhood been sacrificed to
adolescence but even infancy is affected. Babies must suffer the
nutritional and psychological deficiencies of bottle-feeding
because their mothers are terrified of losing their teenage breasts.
At the same time, baby fat is under increasing negative scrutiny.
The new "slim-fit" diapers are the thin edge of a sinister trend.
Some children are being put on diets by their parents while others are encouraged to do aerobic exercise in order to tone and
slim their bodies. Barbie has released an aerobics video for pre-
adolescent girls.

Perhaps the emphasis on the adolescent body-plan is a result
of the American male's predilection for paedophilia. Witness the
socially condoned enthusiasm for Brooke Shields and Nadia
Comaneci. Peculiarly, the optimal female body for heterosexual
American males calls for oversized breasts on a pre-adolescent
frame. This combination is part of a self-perpetuating cosmetic
cycle. The male infatuation with breasts is a direct result of the
lack of breast-feeding in infancy. The largeness recaptures the

proportions they would have experienced orally as infants.

Given their druthers (i.e., total economic freedom), the marital pattern of most Americans would fall into the category of serial monogamy, a markedly adolescent dating behaviour. The inherent narcissism of adolescence ensures that the consciences of multiple divorcees will not be troubled by any negative impact that their lifestyle might have on their children.

INTIMATE
STRANGERS

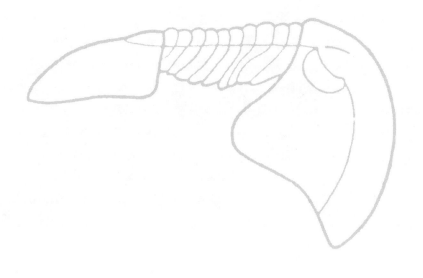

LE

CAPITAL LOVE

---

*O*F SOME LOVERS the world is envious; it would destroy
them out of jealousy. They are spurned and exiled by their
friends. Events conspire against them. They extract so much joy
from the general economy of pleasure that a toll is levied on
everyone excluded by their union. These lovers are a cartel, a
yoke of oppression to be thrown off by the disinherited prole-
tariat of love.

IMPLODED COUPLES

---

*C*ERTAIN COUPLES seem to implode, enhancing and rein-
forcing each other's weaknesses. They fall through themselves into each other. They are spurned because they have
become loathsome to everyone but themselves.

ONLY PARTI
ALITY IS TR
ULY IMPART
IAL

RELATIONSHIPS
AS NEUROTIC

$\mathcal{T}$HERE is a neurotic component to almost all relationships, especially those that develop into an infernal symbiosis, a twisted dependency wherein two individuals hopelessly complicate their own life-trajectories by introducing an additional set of necessities and constraints. This type of dependency is the condoned pathology of our society.

The imploded violence of mutual projections, as well as the intermingling of two unconsciousnesses, creates a tangled, single entity shared by the two partners. Half of their relationship takes place on the unconscious plane, mediated by their mutual identity. Thus, one of the most important influences on each of their lives takes place outside both their consciousness and their ability to do anything about it.

EXTRAMARITAL
RELATIONSHIPS
AND INTUITION

*O*NE of the least-considered casualties of extramarital relationships is intuition. When your intuition tells you that your spouse is having an affair, you will eventually work up enough nerve to ask, "Are you seeing somebody else?" When you ask this you half expect a denial, even though your sixth sense is screaming that the accusation has a foundation. Your partner's standard reply here is a lie camouflaged by feigned indignation—"How could you even think such a thing?"—or intimidation—"You must be the one having an affair."

These accusations and counter-accusations are repeated until finally, through persistence, you learn to mistrust your intuition.

Intuition is a fragile antenna that communicates the inner emotional states of those around us. To damage this faculty is surely a crime.

SEXUAL INTELLIGENCE

*S*EXUAL INTELLIGENCE is sometimes independent of
intellectual capability. The most brilliant minds may have
the sexual alacrity of a dullard, while simple minds may be
equipped with a high degree of sexual sophistication. Sexual skill
is a creaturely cleverness, a kind of orgasmic choreography
orchestrated by the body itself. The natural variation of individual nervous systems means that the collaborative project of rap-
ture suits some humans more than others.

MULTIPLE SUCCESSIVE RELATIONSHIPS AS A VEHICLE TO SELF-TRANSFORMATION

*E*very new relationship has the potential to animate a new aspect of self. It is the nature and power of human attachment to conjure this new self from the centre of what we sometimes take to be stable and finite within us. Sexual intimacy is the catalyst of this transformation. For each person we are intimate with, we are a different person.

At the beginning of a relationship each partner nourishes within the other this new identity. The combination of two separate sets of emotional and intellectual characteristics is equivalent to a genetic blending; however, instead of one person sharing two sets of characteristics there are two new beings, one in each partner. The process is almost chemical. In fact, in the deepest levels of the psyche there may be a drive to self-transformation that, in itself, is responsible for guiding the partners towards each other.

Fully encountering a new being is, therefore, a delightful crisis of identity. It can also be physically addictive, and some individuals become hooked on the tremendous rush of energy exchanged between the two totalities of a couple making love for the first few times, an experience tantamount to the first glimpses of an exotic, unknown land. Each new partner opens up a different interior world in ourselves, and every new identity is imprinted and stored in a personal repository of potentiated identities in the centre of our being. Opportunists can use the energy of these homunculi to enlarge their psyches into a composite source of pure energy.

A TRUTH NO
T GRASPED E
MOTIONALLY
IS NO TRUTH
AT ALL

ENAMORATION—
LOVE AT FIRST SIGHT

*S*OME of those who do not believe in romantic love reduce it to a culturally imposed concept, arguing that it did not even exist before the Elizabethan era.

Romantic love is deeper than the agnostics would have us think, however. In the Munich Museum there is a 2,400-year-old Greek dish depicting the hero Achilles slaying Penthesileia, queen of the Amazons. As he impales her with his spear he is looking into her eyes. According to Greek mythology, at the same moment that he struck the death blow their eyes locked and they fell in love.

Love at first sight is a concomitant of self-consciousness. The ability of two people to lock into each other's existential totality is characteristically human and pan-cultural. Just as to be conscious is to be able to see yourself in a mirror as intimate other, so to be conscious is to be liable to fall in love at first sight.

There is a joyous wisdom to this look that is highly characteristic regardless of the face. It is as if it bears the identity of some universal being who gazes out of various faces. The mesmeric power of this look is almost frightening.

The knowledge that the divine other exists in this world illuminates it. Enamoration is the marvellous secret that loves to go naked, to testify to the world. It is a kind of death because you abandon yourself in the totality of another being.

To love deeply is an exquisite suicide.

INFINITE SEXUAL
VARIATION DURING
LONG-TERM MONOGAMY

$\int$ EX with a single partner over many years has the potential to become increasingly intimate and skillful. There is a subtle faculty deep within us that gradually varies mutual sexuality and ensures the continual elaboration of our appetites and positions. The partners' nervous systems become so sensitive to each other that they become mutually entrained. This resonance, a sexual synchronicity, has the potential to give each orgasm a unique mood and ambience.

The devoted monogamous couple are mutual explorers of a sexual landscape limitless in extent.

AGING
AND SEXUALITY

---

*A*GING is a physiological manifestation of character, an essentializing of musculature. The older adult stands revealed. For this reason slightly dissipated features and vaguely deconstructed bodies can be highly attractive, sexually. Through usage, sexual organs physically evolve into their function, adorned with extra folds and rich, velvet skin, at once delicate and durable. The hair thins, drops away with vanity, leaving a greater, more vulnerable area of skin, a personality disarmed and fully sexual. The softer breasts support giant nipples, eroticized from breast-feeding. Wrinkles around the eyes and mouth become a testimony of experience and a sum of disposition. The hands, worn and smooth with human familiarity, possess an experienced touch, paradoxically childlike in its unexpected tenderness.

THE
PLANET'S
DREAM

LE

THE EXTRICATION
OF SELF

*H*UMAN BEINGS are born spiritually incomplete. Our life task is the acquisition of a unique psychic component, which is necessary for our ontological closure. Traditionally this component is searched for in the domain of religion, psychology and philosophy. However, we will not even be able to recognize it unless we have already achieved individuation. It follows, then, that our primary goal as humans is to disentangle ourselves from our familial and socio-historical matrices until we are standing clear. Imagine not being absolutely sure about even the first two terms of Descartes' *Cogito*.

This process is a self-analysis, a weeding out of the extraneous material we have incorporated into our psyches from an early age. Our assimilated assumptions, biases and dispositions are a formative prosthesis that is, eventually, contradictory to intellectual and emotional objectivity and our project of self-fulfillment. Self-emancipation is a tremendous task and its aim is to remove whatever is not proper to ourselves—the insistent noise of our cultural fictions. In order to achieve it we must first re-enact the evolution of our own culture.

Picking out the threads that have been woven into the fabric of your being is a difficult job. Our culturally inculcated misconceptions are so deeply embedded in the experience of self that to extricate them, to pluck them out, is a painful process requiring ceaseless vigilance. You must be ruthless in the service of your original being.

Philosophical, psychological and religious systems of thought are techniques of individual extrication. They do this by creating systems of exclusion that describe and identify the degree of familial, historical and cultural influences impinging on the original self. The vantage gained by achieving self-individuation carries with it a responsibility to other humans, whose lives are illuminated by this portentous objectivity.

The extrication of self is the politic of perception.

WE ARE SELF-A
BSORBED OBS
ERVERS, STEEP
ED IN THE HY
PNOTIC SPLE
NDOUR OF M
EMORY

CONSCIOUSNESS

*T*HE PHENOMENA of consciousness are maddeningly elusive. Trying to observe the observer is a frustrating form of shadow-boxing. What is even more frustrating is knowing that all the information we need to understand our own consciousness surrounds us at every instant of our lives.

It is staring us in the face, or, more properly, staring out of our faces.

DISOWNING THE SELF

$\mathcal{L}$IKE BATHERS afraid of cool water, most of us are unwilling to explore morally or aesthetically uninhabitable parts of our own psyches. Nearly all of us live our lives without extending into the dark corners of our existences; we are afraid to acknowledge the deviances and neuroses we all harbour. There are also acts we wish to disown, embarrassing or "mistaken" things that we have done. It is this alienation from ourselves that impairs our ability to fully inhabit ourselves, to take responsibility for our totality. We cannot celebrate that which is only piecemeal.

At the same time, our propensity as humans for self-delusion, for being able to accept hackneyed, provisional models of mental phenomena (which include most contemporary psychological notions) is almost infinite. We excel at mesmerizing ourselves, charmed by our own consciousness's facility for inventing plausible rationalizations of behaviour.

RANDOM BEHAVIOUR
AND PERSONAL GROWTH

We are defined, to a degree, by our family and friends. In a relationship, one partner's characterizations of the other can limit the other's potential through over-determination. Sometimes one partner's expectations become so restrictive they cause the other to act precipitately to save him- or herself from a destructive and stereotypical characterization. Sometimes we constrain ourselves, through habit or insecurity, and again we may act heroically in order to break out of our self-definitions. Once you have secured a truly new direction in your life, either by changing circumstances or making a new resolution to achieve your potential, you have an opportunity for real self-transformation.

To engage this new-found freedom you must enact behavioural options randomly at first, simply to initiate self-transformation into areas that you might otherwise not have stumbled. You must deliberately do things that are uncharacteristic of you. By committing these actions, some even nonsensical or crazy, you resensitize yourself to the natural flow of personal choice. This is essential in order to redefine your boundaries and potentials as well as to familiarize yourself with a whole new array of possibilities. By exercising even the zaniest options you facilitate the engagement of freedom.

To become yourself you must become a stranger to yourself.

IN DEFENCE
OF NARCISSISM

---

*N*ARCISSISM is the only tenable existential position. To be narcissistic is to celebrate our miraculous condition, the terrible beauty of our incarnation. We are the only knowable and sacred miracles at hand. Not to love the self spiritually and erotically is a failure of perception and logic. This is why the absolute autonomy of an erotically narcissistic woman, delighted by her own beauty as she dances before a mirror, is such a powerful aphrodisiac. It is this power that makes the narcissist immune to psychoanalysis.

Lou Andréas Salomé, a novelist and psychoanalyst from the turn of the century, called narcissism the "hermaphroditic self-embrace." To her it was the "divine" subsoil that nourished all the phenomena of the self. She claimed that Narcissus' pool was the unconscious and that to lose your narcissism was to become "sterile in body and soul." Narcissism is, then, the ultimate vehicle to a supreme, cosmic unification with the universe as a whole because the narcissist's identification with the universe is so total that, paradoxically, its absolute grandeur is grasped and comprehended.

The existential narcissist, aware of the impermanence of existence, aware that the entire universe will also end one day, does not despair, does not regard life or activity as futile but, rather, in the Dionysian fullness of the moment, each second of which is an eternity, celebrates existence and all its products.

DELUSIONS
OF PRIVACY

---

*O*UR MOST INTIMATE and private emotions, our unconscious moods and dispositions, are sometimes more read-
ily accessible to strangers than they are to spouses, family
members and even ourselves. The reflection of our innermost
realities sometimes awaits us on the street, in the anonymous
crowd. It is there that strangers can tell you who and how you
are, could reveal to you your most personal and subconscious
state of mind, if you would let them. We have an involuntary
confessional broadcast that radiates from our eyes, expression
and body posture, and all of us are latent experts at interpreting
each other's psychological states. It seems that the only thing
that interferes with this process is intimacy, culminating in the
hyper-intimacy of an individual's relation to him- or herself.

THE FICTION
OF IDENTITY

*O*UR IDENTITY is intimately bound up with index memories, which we use to represent ourselves to ourselves. Index memories are long-term memories that seem to exemplify our uniqueness. We see ourselves as individuals who did certain things at certain times, and this is how we reassure ourselves of our personal identity. Our inventory of index memories is usually fairly small; in fact, it represents only a fraction of our total prior existence. (What happened to the rest of this time?)

There is a theory that everything we have ever witnessed or done is recorded in an internal repository, and that on some level (possibly the unconscious) these memories are available to us. Whether or not this comprehensive repository exists does not alter the fact that, on the conscious level at least, our store of memories is so minimal and arbitrary as to render us fictions. Our unique index memories are tantamount to a kind of personal mythology. We are adepts of our own oral histories.

When you are dealing with products of mind such as memory, often as not you are actually dealing, as a subjective observer, with unsubstantiated notions. You assume that your memory is the only thing that stays the same in a constantly changing world. All else may change, but the fact that you did a certain thing at a certain time does not. In reality even memory transforms over time, embellished by your own transformations and mutated by the light of the present. Consider, for example, when you suddenly remember something you thought you had forgotten. A traumatic or unpleasant life experience will sometimes trigger long-forgotten parallels of this experience from your past. It is as if in your current state of mind you have initiated communication with all your prior incarnations who shared the same emotions. We suppress or revise our memories according to our present circumstances.

Furthermore, if self consists of a model that we construct largely out of memory, and if personal memory is hobbled by large discontinuities, then what *is* self? It is full of holes, memory gaps, like an abandoned summer pavilion through which a cool wind blows. If we had to take a history exam about our own lives, citing precise dates and events, we would fail miserably. We entertain extremely vague notions about ourselves. We even incorporate other people's memories into our own, particularly those of family members, probably because in families the border between collective and individual memories is apt to blur.

What we perceive as self is only an aggregate of index memories, appropriated personas and revisionist histories—an almost complete fabrication.

MORALITY AS HANDLE

*M*ORAL CODES impose a series of boundaries and constraints that ensure that, at some point in your life, your
innate behavioural tendencies will come into conflict with their
proscriptions. In some respects, particularly as a consensually
determined method of enforcing interaction, morality is tantamount to an arbitrary system of protocol. This aspect of morality transcends its social function of constraining behaviour for
the good of the species.

Consensual moral systems provide a sort of emotional dock-
ing bay or handle for others to manipulate us according to specific conventions. We are conditioned to operate within moral
systems during childhood. Love and dependence enable the ethical apparatus to be superimposed on our psyches and, once in
place, it becomes of lasting importance in adulthood. In fact,
the moral apparatus seems to become even more entrenched as
we grow older, as if it had some sort of delayed ethical fuse.

Very early in their development, children use their knowledge of moral systems to manipulate adults. By purposefully
challenging parental rules the child tests the adult's tolerance
using his or her knowledge of the morality game. Even if the
interaction proves to be a negative one it still reinforces the
child's status as a player in the game as well as satisfying a deeper
need for meaningful contact. Such behaviour is extended well
into the adult realm. In our most intimate relations our morality
is the handle we provide, almost involuntarily, for others to
hook into us.

THE IMMACULATE
PERCEPTION

---

*D*IFFERENTIATION and isolation of previously mixed elements and their subsequent refining are natural outcomes of our sorting impulse. Humans possess an almost instinctive need to isolate the constituent parts of perceived reality. This impulse led us to discover the hidden numerical order of nature and its properties. It has also got us into trouble. Refined foods such as sugar have imbalanced our nutrition, refined chemicals have poisoned us.

To differentiate an item from its background satisfies the innate aspiration of consciousness towards specificity. Isolation reinforces the identity of the item and establishes its status as signified, an ideal form. It is the enforcement of differentiation. Grouping raises the charge of serial identity; large assemblies of species or metals engendered the first wealth. Refining became a method of harnessing the ritualized impulse to further isolate the constituent parts of reality, the final differentiation. Refining is the fine-tuning of purity towards an ideal isolation tantamount to icon or symbol.

One of the most extreme consequences of the refining impulse is the refinement of uranium, where, as the essence is isolated, the substance being refined becomes increasingly toxic to human life.

SHORT-TERM REALITY

W E ARE temporal entities based in narrative, sequential time. Our short-term memories are specialized to function in very limited periods. Because we operate in the world using generalizations about most things, we don't need the specificity of short-term memory for more than the brief periods we use it. Although what we experience as consciousness is located fully within its compass, short-term memory is more like an evaporating trace than a permanent record.

The next time you visit an unfamiliar building—a hotel in a foreign city, for example—try to recall details of the interior an hour or two afterwards, while in a new environment. You will be surprised at the large sections missing. The colour of the carpets, the sequence of hallways and stairwells will elude you. If the structure of the building deteriorated as fast as your memory of it did, it wouldn't be standing for long.

This fact doesn't stop us, however, from behaving as if all the salient features of a given locale, once visited, are familiar and static thereafter, as if deposited in an archive. In actuality the mnemonic space begins to deteriorate within hours of our exposure to a new location. It is as if the world were transient, in constant phantasmic flux; its details degrade and become amorphous in our absence. This is the inherent reality of the world as we are constantly negotiating it, and yet for the most part it is screened out of our consciousness.

Major components of our everyday, familiar realities can be modified radically without our noticing. We find ourselves trying to unlock the wrong car in a parking lot, we don't notice that a friend has shaved off his mustache over the weekend. The extremely subjective and projective short-term reality we inhabit is constantly being challenged by causality, and the result is an unstable ground of phenomenological anxiety that seemingly contradicts consciousness.

Memory is a disappearing act. Eurydice. The daughter of memory you couldn't look back at to save her life.

HORMONES ARE THE TRANSUBSTANTIATION OF CONSCIOUSNESS

TIME, BEING,
THE WORLD AND
VISUAL AGNOSIA

---

*V*ISUAL AGNOSIA is a neurological affliction that leaves its victims unable to recognize everyday objects. Books, cows, shoes, trees, buildings, faces are all merely enigmatic shapes with no identity. It is a dysfunctional state, and yet to truly understand the world perhaps it is necessary to achieve intentional visual agnosia. This is because our categorical and nominative consciousness stands between us and a primal apprehension of reality.

Additionally, we must strip away the fiction of our own memories as well as our societal conditioning. Pure existence, selfhood without the mediating influence of language, is the closest thing we possess to an immaterial soul. It exists as an infinite radiance, a timeless moment. Because pure being has no chronology and manifests totally in the present, it resembles the unconscious.

Dreams are the result of the conscious fiction of selfhood mutating under the duress of timelessness in the unconscious. The unconscious mind is suffused with the atemporal radiance of the primal self.

Without memory we are an eternal moment of consciousness. Memories are trailing ghosts that tie us to our identities.

FREE WILL

$\mathcal{H}$UMAN CONSCIOUSNESS operates within the margin between chance and determinism, between the causal and the random. Free will is chance harnessed to intention, and is itself at once causal and random.

INCREMENTAL
PHENOMENA

---

*P*EOPLE can accommodate almost anything if it happens gradually enough. Take the partially bald man who grows a fringe of long hair on one side of his head to comb over his bald pate. This is not the ludicrous vanity it appears to be if you consider that baldness doesn't occur overnight. His hairline receded gradually and, just as gradually, he began to comb his hair a little differently each month, each year, to conceal his receding hairline. Eventually, as the central portion of his crown balded entirely, he arrived at the extreme stage we're accustomed to seeing on windy days, where his ungainly length of hair flails wildly in sudden gusts.

Similarly, we can tolerate imperfections or slightly damaged personal belongings provided we are in some way responsible for these defects. Small, indelible stains on clothing, for example, are acceptable to the wearer if they have a personal history. Dents and rust holes in cars, hair loss and aging can all be overlooked because, by and large, we are blind to subjective incremental phenomena.

We are not blind, however, to the incremental phenomena of others. Even if we can put up with our own clothing being slightly frayed or stained, we tend to frown upon equivalently worn clothing on others. And we would never purchase such damaged goods, even second-hand. It is familiarity that breeds contentment.

Not all incremental phenomena are tangible. Some types are purely mental. Anxieties and swallowed disappointments can all gradually increase until high levels of self-doubt and compromise are tolerated. This dross of resignation and worry can mount to levels that, in our youth, we would have found insufferable.

An opening flower is just below the threshold of incremental perception.

LIFE IS THE AR T OF ACCOMO DATING UNR ESOLVED SITU ATIONS

THE DARK SOURCE:
ETHICAL FUEL AND
THE MID-LIFE CRISIS

---

*A*s STARS like our own sun age they go through several distinct phases. These phases are determined by what element is being burned by the nuclear fires in their cores. A young star burns hydrogen; when that runs out it switches to helium and bloats into a red giant. More massive stars consume their helium and then burn through the less efficient fuels—carbon, nitrogen, oxygen, magnesium and finally iron. Because iron is inefficient, the stars become unstable and ultimately explode in a supernova.

In some respects human psyches are like stars; changes in our development are marked by changes in our psychic metabolism. The sources we use for energy as young adults are different from those we use in mid-life. As we mature, our ethical imperative usually becomes more defined, restricting our ability to maintain a moral distance from our actions. (Curiously, this is just when most adults are having affairs and nursing various holdovers from more youthful identities.) Young adults have a much higher tolerance for darkness, or unconventional morality, than their elders do, and consequently they have greater access to dark-source energy.

Historically the transition from young adulthood to mid-life has been more turbulent for males than for females. The dark-source fuels that men draw upon in their twenties and thirties (affairs, abusive relationships, domination in the workplace, addiction, etc.) are highly combustible and unstable. The natural self-transformation of mid-life requires the cleaner-burning, morally light fuel of maturity. When the male psyche abandons its prior fuel sources without informing the ego, the result is the male mid-life crisis.

Suddenly his identity is coasting on empty. This is the point at which he might take up drug or alcohol abuse with a vengeance, or when his behaviour may become erratic—anything to ameliorate his painful consciousness. Unfortunately, a male's heavy investment in his self-image ensures that the momentum of his prior, inappropriate persona is perpetuated or accentuated, even in the face of his self-originated transformation. He clings desperately to his outmoded persona because the ego sees self-transformation as equivalent to death. The male persona is astonished and appalled by the moral mandate of the primal self.

PLAY

*I*N PLAY, an item or place takes on imaginary characteristics and capabilities not strictly proper to it. In the case of an object, its identity is transposed either by its resemblance to an imagined object or by its proximity to an imagined locale. Commonplace items such as brooms or pencils are decontextualized by children and reidentified as relational items in a transposed drama. Thus, a pencil is transformed into a rocket, or a broom into a horse. The floor becomes water, and by permutation of the metaphor, the rugs are islands. The recontextualizing power of the fantasy perfuses the immediate environment of the play area.

Childhood play isn't just role-modelling by pretending to assume a particular identity—a policeman, a super-hero, a doll, an astronaut. Through play, children personify the world by identifying with it. By acting out credible narratives in the roles of nonhuman entities (domestic animals, dinosaurs, or even inanimate objects—vehicles, etc.) children learn the world from the inside out. This identificational ability, more than anything else, exercises the intelligence and cognitive dexterity of the child.

Play also exercises one of our most human traits—the ability to metaphorize the environment. Play is the mutational matrix that generates new prototypes.

STYLE AND
INTELLIGENCE

---

*I*NTELLIGENCE is style, your method of operation, your approach. Intelligence is the connections you choose to make by virtue of your personality or individuality, a disposition towards certain choices. These connections are made amongst whatever body of knowledge you happen to possess. Intelligence is not necessarily the quantitative size of your body of experience or knowledge; rather it is how you manipulate and access this information. To a certain extent it is also how your knowledge is structured relative to itself, in that this structure determines the order of your connections.

ASSOCIATIVE
CONSTELLATIONS
AND MEMORY

*A*N ASSOCIATIONAL network is a context. When we acquire knowledge through particular experiences, our mood at the time flavours our subsequent recollections of that knowledge and consequently the associational constellation derived from it. Our ability to embed these complex, associational narratives of spatio-temporal matrices is a multi-dimensional network for absorbing new information.

Association is a map of experience. It is an experiential terrain, which is grouped as a set, as if it were a building that you have been in once before and have since forgotten, but that, upon revisitation, is easily negotiated by recourse to the original memory. Because our sense of orientation, like our vision, is one of our most precise faculties, it can be used to store information by encoding it in an associational constellation.

Metaphor is the daughter of memory.

GHOSTS

_W_HY, whenever ghosts are portrayed in popular culture, are they often engaged in routine activities? Why are they always trudging up and down stairs and hallways or engaged in menial tasks? Perhaps because ghosts represent not the surviving souls of the dead but rather the vestigial souls of the living.

Ghosts are the sum of all the unconscious actions that an individual performs during everyday existence. Ghosts consist of all those things you do unthinkingly or despite your present circumstances. Ghosts are the culmination of moments stolen from consciousness.

Because inattention is an absence of conscious investment in the present moment, it represents a withdrawal from the real, which, in turn, arrests spiritual development by diverting energy from the real and investing it in a discorporate realm. All of these instances, these points when our consciousness is directed elsewhere, gradually conjure a phantom, a shadow-self who shuffles dimly through our lives, rattling its chains of unconsciousness—the chains that bind it to a being who has not learned to inhabit the present moment completely.

SLEIGHTS
OF MIND

SLEEP AND DREAMING

---

*S*LEEP has four stages, each successive stage being a little deeper than its predecessor. During a normal eight-hour sleep you go through several ninety-minute cycles. In each of these cycles you descend from stage-one all the way to stage-four sleep and then rise again, through stages three and two, back into stage one. Stage one is also known as light sleep and is characterized by rapid eye movements (REM), which indicate dream activity.

Approximately one hour after falling asleep you enter stage four or "deep" sleep, which can last a quarter of an hour or more. This stage is characterized by slow, delta brain waves. After passing some time in stage four you begin to rise until your brain waves approach alpha frequencies, or wakefulness. It is at this point that dreams intervene, perhaps to ensure that sleep continues.

Part of the condition of sleep involves the muscular paralysis of the sleeper, possibly as a precaution against the dreamer acting out dreams. This paralysis, called atonia, is sometimes vaguely sensed by the dreamer and can lead to claustrophobic dreams of paralysis. The breakdown of atonia leads to the acting out of dreams, commonly called sleep-walking.

DREAMS

---

*T*HE RELATIONSHIP between consciousness and dreams is similar to the relationship between a tree's branches and its roots. The only difference is that during the night, the tree of consciousness disappears, and the roots of the unconscious project an immaterial, phantom tree into the night air.

Our minds are so used to being flooded by the causal stimuli of diurnal existence that when those stimuli disappear (when we close our eyes and sleep) a part of our mind continues to look for them. Dreams are a fabrication by that part of the mind that never really sleeps; they are causal narratives built around whatever stimuli are available. These stimuli are the lingering emotions and images that stray out of memory during sleep.

DREAM PHYSICS

*T*HE PHYSICAL characteristics of dreams, independent of their content, suggest that their actions take place in a slightly viscous, particulate medium that has some of the properties of both air and water. The viscosity of the dream medium is evident whenever the dreamer tries to move quickly—to run, for instance, or to throw an object. Furthermore, dreams generally have no temperature. Dream snow has the same texture and temperature as beach sand.

Also, when a dreamer tries to look at a specific object in a dream—if, for instance, you pick up an object and look directly at it, as you would when you were awake—ninety percent of the time the object will begin to mutate and transform. This is an example of the mutational effect of consciousness in dreams, a reversal of the waking mode. It is the narrative engine within all dreams. The examination of dream terrain by consciousness creates the dream.

Dreams are to be experienced primarily in a nonspecific, general way. Their very substance breaks down under scrutiny.

TRANSITIONAL STATES OF CONSCIOUSNESS AT THE VERGE OF SLEEP

WE NEED a few good observers at the edge of sleep. The entire riddle of dreams and their relation to the unconscious awaits someone who can describe the various transitional states of consciousness between waking and sleeping.

One of the few scientists who have researched this transition zone was H. Silberer, an associate of Sigmund Freud's. He tried to build up a vocabulary of dream symbols by studying the translation of verbal notions into images at the edge of sleep. Since then there have been only sporadic attempts at mapping this devolution of consciousness.

As we fall asleep the train of thought is disengaged from the causal, outer world. Our thinking becomes almost purely associative and transforms gradually into a train of images. This associative train is highly suggestive and therefore vulnerable to the emotional content welling up from the the deeper parts of the brain. Emotional content determines whether the dreamer will linger on one subject or go on to another.

At the same time, the interior monologue that accompanies thought diverges from the train of images and degenerates into key words that are only vaguely and paradigmatically related to the images of the proto-dreams. Finally, all of these elements, operating somewhat independently of each other, interact. The products of this interaction are the aleotoric sequences/narratives we know as dreams.

NEUROSES
AND DREAMS

---

*N*euroses are disorders of waking consciousness, not of the whole psyche. Possibly they represent a liability of consciousness, a statistically minor side effect. Since neuroses are so entangled in the general phenomena of self-consciousness, most neurotic symptoms disappear in dreams.

During sleep our consciousness is altered so radically that a diurnal neurosis is no longer relevant. It has been invalidated because the structure to which it was attached, waking consciousness, has disappeared. This accounts for the orthopsychic propensity of dreams and, in a sense, contradicts the psychoanalytic view that dreams are pathological.

CINEMATIC TECHNIQUES AS UTILIZED IN DREAMS

_N_ ARRATIVE CONVENTIONS of television and cinema (voice-overs, cuts to multiple points of view and so on) have introduced new devices into the repertoire of representation in dreams. By mediating content that would otherwise be too traumatic and by invoking material that would have no other means of expression, cinematic techniques give permission to the dreamer to externalize anxiety-producing imagery much as if he or she was watching a film.

For instance, in a dream a figure may turn up who at first appears innocuous. However, a "voice-over" might announce that this person is going to hurt the dreamer. Although the dreamer knows what will happen next (because he or she is, on some level, directing the dream), the sense that the dream is a real situation must be maintained. The frightful transformation of the "innocuous" stranger and the dreamer's "escape" by projecting him- or herself into another viewpoint allows the dream to continue. The ability of the dreamer to use a cinematic technique defers the nightmare and allows the dreamer to resume the essential narrative of the dreamwork.

SLEEP-TALKING, WET DREAMS AND ATONIA

*O*UR ABILITY to talk is a recent evolutionary acquisition. As a consequence, the inhibitory motor-paralysis of atonia, which prevents sleepers from enacting their dreams, does not have as firm a hold on their tongues. This may be why sleep-talking is the most ubiquitous of all the sleep disturbances.

On the other hand, because talking is more of a mental or noetic act, perhaps it is partially exempt from the purely physical restrictions of atonia. Perhaps also, through the inherent nesting abilities of consciousness (our propensity to have dreams within dreams, for example), the limits of atonia can be outflanked by noetic consciousness.

Atonia does not figure in some other disturbances of sleep, however. When, as children, we learn nocturnal continence, it is really a process of gradual domination of the unconscious by consciousness using the imperative of voluntary control.

Because the genitals mysteriously participate in the dream process (men have erections and women's clitorises become engorged), wet dreams represent a marvellous gesture of solidarity with the unconscious.

DREAM NARRATIVES
AND ROCK VIDEOS

*R*OCK VIDEOS with the sound turned off are equivalent to dreams. The narrative that drives a rock video's visual sequences (usually cinematic illustrations of the lyrics) is similar to the narrative process in dreams. In both cases, events seem unrelated until the logic of the emotional narrative is revealed.

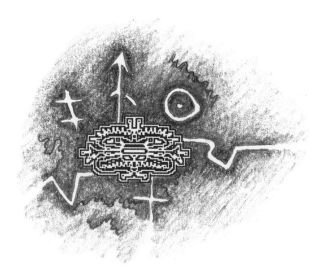

DAYDREAMS

A LARGE PORTION of human consciousness is devoted to planning for future needs. We are speculative creatures who restlessly scan future possibilities. This activity fuels our fantasies and daydreams, which consist of imagined narratives derived from our daily preoccupations. A brief sample from almost anyone's interior train-of-images reveals that we constantly entertain fleeting, hypothetical scenarios, a sort of mental doodling at the edge of our attention. If something is preoccupying us intensely, then certain of these fantasies will become even more vivid. We will go so far as to envisage dreadful eventualities that seem almost masochistic, given the uncomfortable feelings they evoke.

Daydreams and fantasies are directly related to dream material in two ways. Their spontaneous narratives sometimes mimic dream narratives, hence the term "day-dreams," and they occasionally provide seed material for subsequent dreams. The low-key anxiety states that fantasies can provoke are often located at the border of consciousness and consequently slip unnoticed into the unconscious to gestate until they are taken up by dreams.

The greater part of our emotional unconscious consists of unresolved or deferred trains-of-thought which have slipped into the unconscious to simmer on the back-burner of our mind.

THE DISTORTION
OF DREAMS
DURING RECALL

$\mathcal{T}$HE UNCONSCIOUS is timeless, simultaneous and nonlinear. Because consciousness is sequential, causal and narrational it imposes a structure on remembered dreams that is sometimes antithetical to the multi-dimensional reality of the dream itself. Perhaps this accounts for the "fleeting" quality dreams have upon awakening—we experience the peculiar temporality, the nonlinear aspects of the dream only briefly before they vanish, evaporating in the narrative that consciousness imposes on the dream content.

Certainly there are dreams that are very narrative, but even they, when examined closely, have simultaneous elements. The context in which a particular dream takes place can be as rich in detail as any encountered in conscious life. If enough detail is recalled, a remembered dream can be changed in its course. For example, if in a dream you walked down a particular city street and went past an alley, you can, with perseverance, learn to walk in your dream-mind's eye back to that alley and explore it, seeing "new" things there.

In another sense, we impose a sequentiality, a narrative, as soon as we arise, in the very process of "remembering," itself a dynamic reordering of the dream material. To articulate a dream in conscious mode, describing it not just to others but to yourself, is a second-order remaking of the dream, a confabulation that distorts the dream by forcing it into a linear mode alien to its nature. It is as if a time-wind blows out of our eyes and into the dream, displacing the fragile relations of dream components as a gust of autumn wind disturbs the fallen leaves.

Consciousness has a Heisenbergian effect on recalling dreams. A dream's symbology could be said to be flexible according to which narrative is "fixed" during the act of recalling the dream to consciousness. Waking consciousness irons out the dream, flattens it.

GENUINE FAS
CINATION CO
UNTS FOR MO
RE THAN EDU
CATION

DREAMS,
WATER AND THE
UNCONSCIOUS

---

*M*ANY of our common metaphors and dream symbols are
apposite because they originate in the way we experience
the world with our bodies. For example, it is generally held that
bodies of water in dreams represent the unconscious. This seems
particularly apt when we look at some of the entailments of this
metaphor; for instance, when we sleep we are "submerged" in
dreams, during our waking hours the unconscious acts like
"ground water," existing "below" consciousness while the everyday events of consciousness "seep" down into it.

Dream analysis, which includes the daily recording of
dreams and weekly discussions of their content with a dream
analyst, is a way of raising the water level of the unconscious.
Iterating the symbology of dreams during waking hours opens a
portal through which the unconscious leaks into consciousness,
sometimes flooding it (an experience invariably accompanied by
anxiety).

Another aqueous property of the unconscious is demon-
strated by neuroses. Many people live with subclinical, unmani-
fested neuroses. These latent neuroses often consist of all the
repressed anger, unresolved guilts, secret lusts, envy and sadness
of their lives. The unconscious acts as a pool into which the neuroses diffuse. If so much neurotic material is pushed into the
unconscious that it is finally saturated, sleep will become preoccupied with the themes of the neuroses. The magnified neuroses
then go on to manifest as a pathological metaphor, a neurotic
symptom, in the conscious mind. This symptom is a distillation

of the repressed material and can display itself in various modes: hypochondria, phobias, panic attacks, etc.

Because neuroses are mostly a phenomena of waking consciousness, and because the imagery of dreams doesn't generally represent the neurotic material (not openly in any case), the process of neurotic flooding seems to leap-frog over the dream content. The neurotic anxiety is connected to a vigilant part of the sleeper that remains somewhat conscious during sleep. It is this vigilance that begins to affect the therapeutic, escapist capability of the dream state. Insomnia is one of the signs of an unconsciousness becoming steeped in preoccupation with a latent neurosis.

POWER
DREAMS

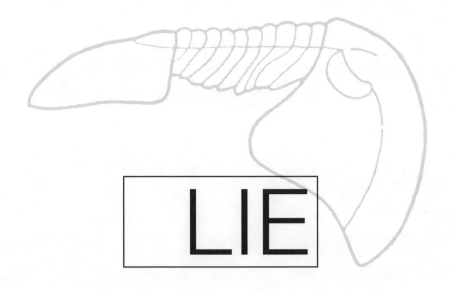

LIE

THE UNCONSCIOUS

---

*T*HERE is no mystery to the unconscious. It consists of all those thoughts, sensations, feelings and memories of which we are not currently conscious. The boundary between consciousness and unconsciousness is not sharply defined. There are some things that we are more conscious of than others, and the margin of consciousness is extendible.

Consciousness is a mobile point of attention that roams the unconscious.

DEMON SHADOW

---

*O*UR DARK SIDES, our shadows, are normally invisible to us. They are entities accustomed to moving parallel and silently through the realm of the unconscious, tracking the activity in our conscious lives. If, by chance, we become aware of them, they sometimes turn malicious.

An exposed, pernicious shadow will occasionally attack the conscious host. Because our demon shadows are an aspect of our personal unconscious, only we can see or be threatened by them. Their attacks usually take place in nightmares. It is the intimacy of the terror that makes such nightmares so frightening.

The demon shadow is often white, for the same reason that Moby Dick was white. In the natural habitat of the shadow, in the waters of the unconscious, white is the colour of terror because it precedes the acquisition of words by the psyche.

The pure voiceless fear of the unwritten page.

COCAINE
AND THE SHADOW

---

*C*OCAINE creates a negative ethical charge in the pool of the unconscious. With enough usage this charge floods the entire unconscious in an excitatory diffusion, a net of pure, unresolved need. Cocaine whets the appetite for spiritual experience that it cannot provide. It is a simulacrum of desire, an artificial sweetener that leaves a bitter taste in the psyche while supplying no real nourishment for the soul.

It is this lack of psychic sustenance that develops the negative charge. The pool of the unconscious breeds a shadow, a psychic golem, a malign homunculus, a nether being who enacts the revenge of unsatisfied spirituality. Witness the sudden, furious behaviour of the cocaine abuser. It is the irrational rage of a mindless, libidinous monster.

PERIPHERAL VISION
AND THE
UNCONSCIOUS

---

*M*OST OF US, in our daily lives, have experienced fleeting hallucinations. Almost everyone has had a brief misperception, momentarily seeing, for example, an article of discarded clothing as the family pet. Misreadings of text are another instance of the same phenomenon. The periphery of vision is much more active than we think.

The visual periphery is the optical correlate of the unconscious. The "corners" of our eyes are a portal into the subconscious mind. It is as if the unconscious perfuses our peripheral vision during waking hours, biding its time like nocturnal animals gathered at the entrance to a cave, waiting for darkness, when they will emerge to dominate the entire visual field.

Sometimes a cave animal steps boldly into the full sunlight of consciousness.

SINISTER
DETERMINISM

---

*T*HERE IS an insistent, disturbing, almost malefic component to both Freudian and Jungian analysis. This hidden agenda is the notion of psychic determinism, which is held to be axiomatic and which makes an individual accountable for every conscious and unconscious action he or she makes.

It is widely held in psychoanalytic circles that there are no accidents, there are no mistakes. Industrial injuries and automobile accidents are a manifestation of destructive urges, and as such are actually varieties of criminal negligence, particularly when they involve innocent victims. Thus Jung could blithely accuse a mother whose children died of typhus after she bathed them in tainted water of murder, and Freud could state that every gratuitous error of speech concealed an intention.

The ramifications are staggering. The homicidal culpability of the automobile driver involved in an accident pales in comparison to the notion of the unconscious suicide. Individuals who might consciously perceive themselves as well adjusted, amiable and cheerful, and be regarded as such, could in reality, underneath their conscious patina of healthy optimism, be harbouring a depressive, maniacal or even suicidal id trying to fling itself (and its attendant ego) into the abyss of annihilation. Conversely, unconscious homicidal/suicidal sociopaths could be walking among us unnoticed, could even *be* us.

Psychic determinism places us in a paranoid position, where if we don't acknowledge the unconscious, "it" could do something "we" might regret. Acceptance of the notion of psychic determinism is like being held hostage by a diabolical terrorist who can be detected only by being materialized incrementally

89

before your eyes during psychoanalysis. It certainly obliges you to undergo analysis as a psychic prophylaxis against unconscious violence. But even with analysis you run the risk that your psychoanalytic journey, doing a slow dissolve on your current reality, will bring you into a new reality even more frightening, where you are more culpable for dark forces and strange sexualities.

It is a double bind. Psychoanalysis must continue its mandate—the annexation of the unconscious—for, according to the doctrine of psychic determinism, the unanalyzed are a danger to themselves and society.

PARANOID
SCHIZOPHRENIA

$\mathcal{P}$ARANOID SCHIZOPHRENIA is essentially an elaborate personal cosmology (bearing the hallmarks of ad hoc rationalization). At the onset of an episode there is usually a triggering event that skews the entire subjective reality of the psychotic individual. The paranoid system develops out of this original displacement of reality and ramifies through the whole of the victim's universe, like an off-register print. Even if the original displacement is only one decimal point to the left or right of reality, so to speak, then the afflicted person is as removed from consensual reality as if the displacement were a hundred percent. He is then faced with the task of trying to map and reregister his new, involuntary cosmology with the observed world—a sisyphian and usually hopeless task. His interpretations will exhibit his personal characteristics; if he is a lawyer, then his confabulations will have a quasi-legalistic air to them.

Because the ontological dilemma of the paranoid is projected into a cosmology, and because this alienation is detected by him in all aspects of reality, delusions of reference inevitably arise. It is only natural for afflicted individuals to conclude that the perceived consistency of their hallucinatory realm could only be so if it were centred on them. Even the most logical of paranoid schizophrenics (if those terms are not mutually exclusive) will gradually convince himself of his concentricism, so overwhelming will the evidence appear to be.

Given this apparently miraculous solipsism, the afflicted individual's task is hermeneutical; he must find out the code of the mystery. Consequently, messages are heard on radios and televisions, and every small gesture and nuance, even incidental phenomena, take on signifying or symbolic functions. Everything conspires in the ontological dilemma. This state of mind is the opposite of satori, where the autonomy of the self is merged into the ultimate autonomy of the universe.

Also, there is a frantic sense of contingency driving the schizophrenic's hermeneutical search, a desperation that leads to insomnia, disordered thinking and labile emotional states. These, in turn, eventually burn out the psyche and flatten the emotional affect due to neurotransmitter depletion and pathological changes in neurological function. All this is a result of the victim's attempt to attain the unrealizable goal of reconciling his involuntary cosmology with consensual reality, a task requiring superhuman devotion, energy and intelligence.

There have been instances, however, where individuals have completed the paranoid's hermeneutical task. Daniel Paul Schreber, a paranoid schizophrenic of Freud's time, was able, eventually, to reconcile his first psychotic episode through tremendous intellectual exertion. Perhaps his task was aided by the fact that his original displacement remained fairly stable so that he could operate within his delusional system while also orienting within consensual reality.

A REINTERPRETATION OF FREUD'S DREAM OF "IRMA'S INJECTION," THE PHENOMENON OF INVOLUNTARY RUMINATION IN MEMORY RECALL, FLIESS, TURBINATE BONES, AND FREUD'S PSYCHOSEXUAL THEORY OF THE NEUROSES

WHILE he was a student, Freud witnessed a public demonstration of hypnotism given by Hansen, a well-known mesmerist. Freud was fascinated by the trance state assumed by the subject, particularly the subject's pale complexion. This pallor not only verified the hypnotic state but also provided a traumatic point of reference for Freud's own unconscious apprehension of what, for him, was a vaguely anxiety-provoking scene. More than a decade later a reference to this paleness arose again in at least two of his dreams, which were used as examples in *The Interpretation of Dreams.* One of the dreams concerned his colleague Fliess, while the other focused on a patient of his, Irma. It is in relation to the second dream that the traumatic pallor of the hypnotized subject whom Freud witnessed as a student played an important role.

In the dream ("Irma's Injection" as it is referred to in *The Interpretation of Dreams*) Freud and a professional colleague examined the interior of Irma's mouth. This was after Freud had noticed that both Irma and his colleague were unusually pale—a reference back to the hypnotic episode and an indication that, at a certain level, Freud still hadn't resolved or integrated the trauma of manipulating other human psyches by hypnotic suggestion.

(Unresolved traumatic incidents, or incidents representative of a stressful period in one's life, can emerge in dream material weeks, months or even years after the event. These unresolved memories may be characterized by a locale, or by some relationship of the actors within the dream or they may be condensed into a single sign, such as paleness in this instance. Such signs resonate in the unconscious long after the original stimulus. It might be that they are used as "class referents"—psychic symbols for a larger group of phenomena, which stand in for some contemporary concern of the dreamer's.

(There might also be some mechanism of periodicity that represents this material to the unconscious mind in recognizable cycles or periods of time after the original event—two months, one year, four years, etc.* A cycle of upwelling memories is part of a larger memory-discharge mechanism essential to human consciousness. It is evident at an early age. Toddlers often spontaneously remember an event that has no associative tie to any

---

* In Freud's time a researcher by the name of M. Swoboda proposed that there was an eighteen-hour period between an incident and its appearance as "day residue."

present activity. There seems to be an automatic, involuntary ruminative mechanism in humans that constantly presents memories in a random manner. It is out of these oblique connections, the juxtaposition of random recall with our current reality, that we fashion true intellectual originality as adults.)

The dream of Irma's injection also refers to Freud's relationship to Fliess, as the turbinate bones that Freud and Fliess discover at the back of Irma's mouth (in Freud's dream) imply. In fact, *this* is the central focus of the dream; the examination of Irma's mouth reveals that she has turbinate bones (normally in the nose) at the back of her mouth. These nasal structures were important for both Freud and Fliess, particularly Fliess, as they were at the centre of his dubious theory of sexual arousal and menstrual cycles. Basically Fliess believed that there was an intimate connection between the genitals and the nasal passages and that operations to cauterize the turbinate bones in the nose would effect changes in other, more psychic phenomena. Both Freud and Fliess operated on Freud's early patients, cauterizing their turbinate bones, sometimes with wildly deleterious consequences, one woman (possibly Irma herself) almost dying from the procedure.

Perhaps cauterization of the turbinate bones was viewed by Freud and Fliess as a sort of prophylactic against genital arousal and basal instincts in general, the way some societies view clitorectomy. There was definitely a connection between women, menstruation, the turbinate bones, genitals, sex and hysteria in their notions; in Freud's case deliberations found their way into some of his aetiologies, particularly his proposed psychosexual genesis for the origin of the neuroses.

It seems not unreasonable to conclude that one possible interpretation of the turbinate bone sequence of the dream is a thinly disguised allusion to the relationship between Fliess and Freud. In the dream perhaps the colleague is Fliess and the two of them are examining their "mutual" patient (the projected condensation of the homoerotic component of their relationship?) whose "mouth" (read genitals) contains the infamous turbinate bones that had preoccupied Freud and Fliess for so long.

What verifies this interpretation is the fact that Fliess operated on Freud's turbinate bones that very summer to try to intercede in a recurrent nasal infection that was probably mostly to blame on Freud's cigar smoking and cocaine use. Fliess cauterized Freud's turbinate bones. There is a direct, causal relation between the turbinate bones, as Freud envisaged them in the dream projected into the sexually displaced orifice of the deathly pale, hypnotic/hysterical woman, and the eventual emergence of his theory of transference and counter-transference, which had its roots in the use of hypnotism in his own practice from December 1887 to March 1889.

PROJECTIVE
CONVERGENCE
AND CROWDS

*M*UCH is made of Jung's concept of synchronicity. Many interpret it as an endorsement of belief in magical processes. It is probably a moot point as to whether Jung himself conceived of synchronicity as a form of magic. It would be more accurate to say that synchronicity is an obfuscating term for projective convergence. In other words, the uncanny coincidences described as synchronistic are really events that we have been looking for, perhaps subconsciously, and of which we are, in certain respects, the architects.

This does not diminish the personal value of these events, particularly in terms of their ability to focus our attention on critical changes within ourselves. Projective convergence is especially persuasive when anima or animus figures are mediating important transformational junctures in our lives and need to be materialized in order to catalyze psychological growth.

The more people you are exposed to, the more the likelihood of someone resembling or "incarnating" your anima or animus of the moment. Statistical enlargement can enhance projective convergence.

EMOTIONAL
GYROSCOPES

---

*T*HE PSYCHOLOGICAL equilibrium of a person is similar to a spinning object, such as a gyroscope, that has a steady rate of spin. If outside forces act to increase or decrease the rate of spin (the spin being equivalent to psychic energy) then, like a spinning top, psychological equilibrium can develop a precessional wobble due to the change in its angular momentum. Some individuals are especially susceptible to the effects of criticism or, conversely, of flattery. The latter's effect is more insidious because it can exaggerate a precessional wobble dangerously. Just as spending levels always rise to meet income, so does self-aggrandizement automatically expand the ego to any new perimeter defined by flattery. This is why notoriety is so destructive for certain people.

POWER DREAMS

1. The Royal Road to the Unconscious

IN THE SUMMER of 1895 Sigmund Freud and his family leased a summer residence in a converted entertainment hall on the outskirts of Vienna. The building, called Schloss Belle Vue, sat atop a hill and commanded a pleasant vista. There, during the night of July 23–24, Freud had a dream that changed the course of modern psychology. This was not due to any particular merit of the dream itself, which was commonplace enough, but because Freud was ripe for the insights that the dream illustrated. And it was this dream, the famous "Irma dream," that made Freud later remark that a marble tablet should be affixed to Belle Vue reading: "In this house on July 24th, 1895, the secret of dreams was revealed to Dr. Sigmund Freud."

The dream devolved on a troubling case he had interrupted for the summer holidays. He had had a low-grade dispute with "Irma," his analysand, just prior to the summer break and this unresolved conflict formed the bulk of the dream's content. In it, "Irma" seemed to be suffering some sort of organic malady connected to malpractice by a colleague of his.

This dream proved to be the exemplar in which Freud saw the most lucid evidence he had yet come across of the motivation of dreams, namely wish fulfillment. It consequently became the cornerstone of his book *The Interpretation of Dreams*, which in turn was the key work of his entire psychology—psychoanalysis.

In terms of his subsequent career it is evident that this dream was what North American native peoples used to call a "power

99

dream." The ancient Algonkian had a tradition of dream-fasting, where a young Algonkian would have his *manitou* revealed to him in a special dream after several days of deprivation. The manitou would act as his guardian, and its attributes would thereafter define his identity. Similarly, Freud's dream demarcated his communion with the unconscious and, at another level, signified his betrothal to the id.

The metaphor of marriage is not untoward, for less than three years after this dream, when he was forty-one, Freud ceased sexual relations with his wife and became celibate for the rest of his life.[1] His vows of spiritual devotion, motivated by a Darwinian notion of self-transcendence, necessitated that he break human, fleshly relations. In a sense he had remarried and fused with his dream anima, which from then on took the form of an intellectual incubus, the muse of insight.

The Darwinian Contract

Freud's personal project of self-transcendence through self-analysis also presupposed a moral direction to the assimilation of the unconscious by the pre-conscious, in order to place the unconscious more within the scope of the ego and therefore consciousness. His self-analysis was the method to reach this goal. He felt that this Darwinian alchemy of the soul could transmute the baser metals of the psyche into alchemical gold.[2] On a personal level he believed that this task required vows of sexual abstinence, the celibacy demanded by a jealous goddess. Much like Newton's renowned abstinence years before, he was keeping his body pure, a perfect instrument for divinity.

When *The Interpretation of Dreams* was published in 1900 it was read avidly by a twenty-five-year-old psychologist, Carl Jung. Jung, somewhat of a prodigy, was already assistant staff physician to the director of the Burgholzli, the prestigious and immense psychiatric clinic in Zurich. Freud's book must have been revelatory for him. He wrote to Freud immediately, and after a sporadic correspondence spanning two years he began to practise psychoanalysis at the Burgholzli in 1902. Thus, when the two men met for the first time in 1907, Jung had already garnered six years of first-hand psychoanalytic knowledge. They must have also shared a tremendous intellectual affinity because at that first meeting they talked nonstop for thirteen hours!

Over the next two years their friendship expanded into a highly productive mutual exploration of the psyche. They shared a theoretical and filial rapport unequalled amongst their peers, Jung becoming not only a son to Freud but his equal. Their relationship remained productive and intimate until 1909, when undercurrents began to manifest themselves in several bizarre and unusual incidents.

2. *The Bremen Incident*

In 1909 both Freud and Jung were invited to give lectures at Clark University in the United States. Freud had been allotted five lectures, Jung three. These lectures would turn out to be nothing less than the introduction of psychoanalysis to North America, today represented by a large and powerful psychoanalytic community. Obviously the occasion was a momentous one and, in terms of their careers, it was an exceptional moment of recognition. They had become emissaries of the unconscious. Accompanying them was Sandor Ferenczi, Freud's most valued adviser.

On August 20, Freud arrived at the German port of Bremen, where Jung and Ferenczi awaited him. Before they left the next day aboard the *George Washington,* a strange encounter took place at a luncheon that Freud hosted for his two colleagues. Apparently Jung was expounding at some length on the subject of mummified peat-bog corpses from northern Germany. As he was speaking, Freud became visibly agitated, showing more and more vexation and uneasiness. Finally, he interrupted Jung with the accusation that Jung wanted his death. Jung replied, somewhat incredulously, that he found this an odd interpretation. Whereupon Freud fainted.

The Diagnosis

This cathartic incident, a catastrophe of Freud's vulnerability, marked all of Freud and Jung's subsequent relations with each other. For Jung it was a revelation of Freud's demon, the manifestation of hidden components in Freud's psyche. For Freud it became a potentially embarrassing occurrence with ambivalent repercussions. Perhaps the two men read more into it than was actually involved.

Rationalizing the event later with his colleagues, Freud attempted to maintain his acerbic honesty while trivializing his collapse, attributing it to the combination of mild exhaustion, alcohol and some "psychogenic elements." Eventually he went into these elements in some detail, averting the quickly gathering storm of psychoanalytic attention. His official diagnosis explained the faint as an attack of guilt anxiety, a sort of catharsis brought on by the successful suppression of a "rival" (whom it became increasingly obvious Jung was). Earlier in the Bremen luncheon he had coerced Jung into having a drink. He believed he had been overcome by paradoxical emotions as a reaction to his "little victory" over the teetotalling Jung.

Could Freud's parry of the psychoanalytic communities' anticipated speculations be viewed as a desperate, ill-conceived defensive strategy by someone who, as we find out later from Jung, "cannot risk [their] authority"? Or was it a *calculated* deflection of speculation? By claiming psychoanalytic immunity as it were, being "above" partiality, Freud waived conflict-of-interest accusations and presented his own case. He acted as his own counsel as well as holding the evidence for the prosecution, a position of some considerable advantage.

3. *The Voyage of the* George Washington

If the course of modern psychology since 1900 can be likened to an expanding universe such as Hubble projected for the physical universe in 1926, then the crack that eventually divided the psychological universe—polarizing it into Jung and Freud, night and day—began aboard the *George Washington* as it steamed towards North America. Perhaps both men had intuited this dichotomy at Bremen, but its eventuality was far from their conscious minds during the transatlantic passage.

At the point of sailing, Jung was thirty-four. Tall, erudite and witty, he was Freud's chosen heir, the Anglo-Saxon successor to Freud's psychoanalytic empire. Freud, sensing the menacing climate of racial theory in Europe, hoped that Jung, as an Aryan, would exonerate psychoanalysis as a universal science, not simply a Jewish one. Freud was fifty-three and consolidating the corpus of psychoanalytic procedure, trying to secure its basic tenets against the inevitable counter-theories that he knew would degrade its effectiveness. He was a patriarchal figure, trying to establish the criteria within which psychoanalysis (his embodied psyche) would survive with all his essential precepts intact. He had fought for this goal and would continue to fight tirelessly for decades. The invitation to America was his vindication and crowning success.

The Marathon Group Analysis

The entire foray to Worcester and back took seven weeks, during which time, according to Jung, he and Freud analyzed each other's dreams daily. The most intense period of mutual analysis seems to have taken place during the eight days aboard the *George Washington*, in the intimate, distraction-free and psychologically claustrophobic proximity of a self-propelled island. The ambience was artificially heightened by the momentous and exhilarating circumstances surrounding the voyage, as well as by the physical novelty of a transatlantic trip, the first for both men.

Freud was surprised and gratified to discover, once on board, that the ship's steward was reading his most recently published book, *The Psychopathology of Everyday Life*. Yet with all these outward signs of success he was still committed to the painful trajectory of his self-analysis. It was in this spirit that he participated in the mutual dream-analysis, trying to exhaust all the possibilities of his own psyche in the never-ending quest for latency. On the other hand, the same impulse towards privacy that censored parts of his own dreams as recounted in *The Interpretation of Dreams* was still paradoxically manifesting itself in the context of the mutual analysis, as Jung was to discover one day during a confrontation he had with Freud about a dream Freud related to him.

Authority

The dream involved a "problem" (as Jung referred to it in his subsequent memoirs) that Jung felt required more personal details from Freud's private life in order to illuminate. At this suggestion Freud's demeanour transformed, and looking at Jung with arch suspicion he declared, "But I cannot risk my authority!"

Jung subsequently made much of this statement. He felt that he lost respect for Freud at that instant because it seemed to him that Freud placed his personal authority (linked to his privacy and perceived vulnerability) above truth. Surely, however, it was more of a tribute to Freud's humanity that he would attempt the indefensible, that is, admitting his own grandiosity, his overly personal identification with his psychoanalytic project. Nonetheless, it strategically maintained the sacrosanct integrity of the psychoanalytic project.

All that aside, we can only speculate about the nature of the original "problem" that Jung, with honourable circumspection, declined to reveal in his memoirs. There are a number of candidates for this "problem," two in particular, that are well known. One is the perceived homosexual component of Freud's male relationships, which mildly troubled him, though even Freud admitted more was made of this than it actually warranted. The other is his numerological phobia, of which he had complained to his colleagues on previous occasions and which had given him considerable anxiety.

Jung's Dream

Archaeologists were the heroes of their time. They initiated the ascendancy of the human sciences, which in the first half of the twentieth century were to have their own classical period with men like Freud and Franz Boaz. The identification that both Freud and Jung had with the Egyptologists is discernible in many aspects of their lives, and its indelible contours are very evident in Jung's dream aboard the *George Washington*.[3]

In this dream Jung was exploring a large old house, descending from the second floor to the ground floor and then to the basement. Each level seemed to be furnished from increasingly older eras of human history. In the basement he discovered a trap-door leading to a prehistoric tomb filled with pottery and human skulls, and it seemed he had made a momentous discovery. Here the dream ended.

The image of the Egyptologist, lantern in hand, stumbling upon a forgotten treasure is highly recognizable in this dream, as is the Darwinian notion of strata as Jung descends through evolution to a primitive prehistory. Pondering the dream later (he analyzed it for almost a year), Jung formulated his doctrine of the collective unconscious, one of the keystones of his own psychology, called analytical psychology. Clearly it was his power dream, and he had dreamed it under the very nose of his great colleague and adviser, Sigmund Freud!

Analyzing it the next day, Freud insisted that it belied death wishes towards someone, possibly someone Jung was closely associated with. Jung privately disagreed but was wary of arguing the point. He acquiesced to Freud's implication and suggested his own wife as a possible target of this perverse wish. Freud said that was probably exactly correct.

In actuality the dream was the realization of a fantasy that Jung later incorporated into his theory of the collective unconscious. In his dream he was the heroic archaeologist who, using Darwinian precepts, discovered the ancient sources of the psyche. Furthermore, Jung's dream also referred back to the Bremen incident. In his luncheon digression he apparently had had some confusion between the peat-bog corpses from northern Germany and the mummies purported to be in the lead cellars of the city of Bremen. The dream, then, can be seen as a response to Freud's collapse. There is a direct correlation between the cellars of Jung's Bremen exposition and the cellars of his dream, which occurred less than a week later.

Internecine Conflict:
Freud and Jung Bicker at the Rails

As the *George Washington* entered the New York harbour on the evening of August 27 Freud and Jung stood on the deck. Freud turned to Jung and said, "Won't they get a surprise when they hear what we have to say to them!" Jung, moralistically disinclined to implicate himself in this conspiratorial glee, replied flatly, "How ambitious you are." Freud, indignant, responded,

"Me? I'm the most humble of men, and the only man who isn't ambitious!" to which Jung replied dryly, "That's a big thing—to be the only one."[4]

4. The Munich Collapse

The expedition to America was a tremendous success for both men. However, it was the beginning of a progressive deterioration of their relationship. This increasingly untenable situation, distinguished by many arguments and reconciliations, was dramatized by an occurrence three years after the voyage of the *George Washington*.

In Munich, on November 24, 1912, Freud and Jung marked a temporary rapprochement with a luncheon at the Park Hotel attended by several colleagues, including Freud's biographer, Ernest Jones. During the meal Freud and Jung engaged in a speculative conversation about an Egyptian king called Amenophis IV, who was believed to be the architect of the first monotheistic religion. The conversation turned into an argument, which focused on Jung's objection to an Oedipal interpretation of Amenophis's actions. One of Freud's protégés at the table asserted that Amenophis erased his father's names from all steles and monuments during his reign because of his negative feelings towards his father, and that the monotheistic religion subsequently created by Amenophis was, at its roots, the result of a father complex. Jung, irritated, replied that the destruction of the father's name had nothing personally to do with the pharaoh's father but was rather a sign of Amenophis's dedication to his new religion. Jung explained that, at any rate, this practice of erasing fathers' names from steles was common with other pharaohs also; it was simply a traditional aspect of the culture of the period. At that moment Freud slipped off his chair, collapsing unconscious unto the restaurant floor.

Everyone at the luncheon arose and gathered around the prone figure of Freud. Jung picked him up and carried him in his arms to a sofa in an adjacent room. As he was being carried, Freud came to briefly and looked up at Jung in a swoon, "as if I were his father," Jung later recalled. Upon recovering consciousness Freud remarked, "How sweet it must be to die."

The Diagnosis

Afterwards Freud analyzed his fainting attack as having been provoked by "psychogenic elements" compounded by stress. Furthermore, he had had a sleepless night and had drunk some wine during the luncheon. Basically it was the same rationalization he employed to explain the Bremen incident, three and a quarter years previous. But, as other observers have pointed out, the central topic of the conversation played a much more significant role than any of the protagonists had envisaged.

Freud's identification with the heroic aspects of the Egyptologist can be adduced from the number of Egyptian artefacts displayed prominently in his consulting room—the inner sanctum of psychoanalysis. He had a great passion for things Egyptian. His essay *Moses and Monotheism*, written towards the end of his life, is at once the ultimate expression of his identification with Egyptians and a belated rebuttal of Jung's assertion in Munich. In *Moses and Monotheism* Freud debunks the literal interpretation of biblical history, particularly the Jewish migrations, and hypothesizes that Jews were originally a breakaway sect of Egyptians. On one level this essay reinforces his aversion to religion as superstitious and regressive, and yet on another level it seems to identify Moses as the Egyptian patriarch of the Jewish people.[5]

Freud and Jung's intense identification with archaeology played a central role in their confrontation in Munich. They were arch rivals of psycho-archaeology, each purporting to be discovering their own pharaoh's crypts in the same pyramid. In a letter to Ernest Jones written several days after the Munich collapse Freud brought up another contributing factor (an architectonic influence, perhaps), saying, "I cannot forget that six and four years ago I suffered from very similar though not such intense symptoms *in the same room of the Park Hotel*"[6] (italics mine). This admission, rather than clarifying anything, seems to add another layer of complexity. If Freud is talking about two separate fainting attacks or near-faints then it brings the number of public faints to four. His casual mention of two previous incidents is extremely unusual unless his reference to the one "four years ago" is not a separate occasion but a confusion with the Bremen incident. Even so, that still leaves the collapse of six years earlier to explain. Apparently Freud had fainted under similar circumstances "in relation to" Wilhelm Fliess at least once, though possibly twice. Fliess was, for Freud, very much Jung's predecessor, and his relationship with Fliess was as ambivalent as it was with Jung, satisfying Freud's self-confessed need for close friends who were also adversaries.

The total number of public collapses, then, is at least two, though possibly as many as four. Possibly one "in relation to" Fliess in 1908,[7] one with Jung in 1909, as well as one conceivably "in relation to" Fliess in 1906 (the year of their final, bitter correspondence and, coincidentally, the eve of Freud and Jung's first meeting) and the final episode with Jung in 1912.

5. Jung's Heresy

The reconciliation of Freud and Jung lasted almost a month, but their alienation was so profound that their best efforts could not head off the final rupture, which came about as a result of a scathing letter that Jung sent to Freud in response to Freud's commentary on a previous letter of Jung's. In this prior letter Jung had apparently made an error, a classic Freudian slip that seemed to belie some hostility towards Freud. Jung was outraged at being interpreted thusly (though contemporary analysts would justifiably agree with Freud's assessment) and sent Freud the angry letter that effectively ended their association for all time.

Interestingly enough, in the letter containing the fateful slip, Jung defended himself against an observation Freud had made about Jung's theory of the incest complex, which Freud likened to Adler's theory. Freud had made this comment several months earlier as well, and it had obviously simmered in Jung's mind for some time before his own response. As it happened, Jung's slip occurred in conjunction with the point of highest emotional affect in his letter, in the very sentence where he disavowed affiliation with Adler. Instead of writing "even Adler's cronies do not regard me as one of theirs," Jung transposed a capital letter for the smaller case in German and wrote "even Adler's cronies do not regard me as one of *yours*" (italics mine). The letter was dated December 18.

The crack that had appeared aboard the *George Washington* had now widened into an unbridgeable chasm—psychoanalysis just wasn't big enough for the both of them. The parturition of Jung's analytic psychology (a simple transposition of psychoanalysis) from the Freudian mainstream was a cataclysmic event, the casting out of the archangel. Fromm, Ferenczi and all the others pulled their wagons in a circle and guarded the home fire of psychoanalytic orthodoxy from the savages of the unconscious who had claimed one of their own. Jung had become a dangerous heretic, and he was excommunicated from psychoanalysis forever.

The Wet Master and the Dry Master

In reality Jung was running with the natives. He'd left the psychoanalytic landing party and refused to return back aboard ship at evening call. His sensual propensity for immersion in the baroque complexities of the human unconscious was both fascinating and revolting to the men aboard the landing craft. A voracious consumer of anthropological and mythological data, he was designed for this exploration of the territory Freud had discovered previously, just as Freud was poised to act upon Breuer's discoveries of twenty years before. Jung was condemned, of course, because the knowledge he was gaining appeared to have no practical value and was perceived as totally subjective. It was as if he began to run ahead of the pack, scenting out enigmas and mysteries much further up the trail while discovering pathways into human personality and the ritual necessities of the individual.

But not only did Jung continue to explore Freud's territory, he went on to make his own equally important discoveries. The collective unconscious, the anima and the animus, the archetype and many other terms are now a part of our collective psychology.

Freud, who for whatever reasons wanted to dictate the terms of the exploration of the unconscious for the first hundred years or so, had to watch helplessly from the conductor's podium as a whole section of his orchestra broke into a new anthem.

References

1. *The Denial of Death*, Ernest Becker, pg. 119
2. *Freud: The Man & The Cause*, Ron Clark
3. *Freud: Political and Social Thought*, Paul Roazen, pg. 180
4. *Freud: The Man & The Cause*, Ron Clark
5. *The Life and Work of Sigmund Freud*, Ernest Jones
6. From the letters of Sigmund Freud
7. From the letters of Sigmund Freud

PSYCHOANALYTIC
PIONEERS WHO
LOST THEIR MINDS

A SIGNIFICANT number of the original group of psychoanalysts—some of whom were members of Freud's inner
circle—developed psychotic symptoms and suicidal depres-
sions. Like the radiation sickness that struck the first physicists
who worked on nuclear fission, early psychoanalysts developed
the same symptoms that their science was supposedly curing.
Could it be that the instrument of psychoanalysis was itself so
disruptive, so inexact, that it exacerbated minor neuroses into
full-blown psychoses?

The list of early psychoanalysts who went mad and/or committed suicide is impressive. Otto Gross ended his life by committing a murder/suicide after developing schizophrenia. Victor
Tausk, a psychoanalytic dissenter, eventually committed suicide
after years of torment and depression. Sandor Ferenczi, a one-
time close friend of Freud, became a bitter, alienated dissenter
from the ranks of psychoanalysts. Otto Rank had a major breakdown, and H.W. Frink developed psychosis during the course of
his own psychoanalysis.

NIETZSCHE'S DOCTRINE OF THE ETERNAL RETURN

---

*F*RIEDRICH NIETZSCHE conceived his vision of the eternal recurrence in August 1881 near Sils-Maria in the Swiss Alps. There is nothing intellectually complicated about the doctrine of the eternal return. It asks us to entertain the notion that the present moment we are in, with all its minutiae, we will return to in the future, not just once but innumerable times, and that we will have to live our lives over and over. It is a compelling notion because it makes life an infinite prison of predetermination, where every action has eternal ramifications. Also, the doctrine both exhausts the present moment and somehow estranges us from it.

If, even briefly, you imagine the doctrine in all its disturbing magnificence the effect can be devastating. Nietzsche found the idea frightful at first and only learned to reconcile himself to it by resolving to accept it joyfully.

In essence, the doctrine of the eternal return is a kind of malign Zen koan, a meditational concept that you can apply to your life. Because it is so extreme, it absolutely relativizes whatever you choose to illuminate with it. The almost neurotic perniciousness of this cosmic idea makes it like a software virus for human consciousness. Once you have been exposed to it, it becomes almost self-perpetuating. The doctrine of the eternal return is a test of psychological strength; trying to contain it is an existential task for the human spirit.

Emotionally, the effect of the doctrine is similar to a neurochemical substance. It is the fire that Nietzsche used to burn away nonessential emotions and beliefs. It also represented a phobic fixation for Nietzsche, however, and presaged later difficulties, which were to manifest six years later in his complete breakdown. The doctrine of the eternal return demarcated the border between inspiration and pathology that was Nietzsche's ultimate inheritance.

GROUND
OF THE
IDEAL

LIFE

EDITOR AS
PSYCHOTHERAPIST

*T*HE PROCESS of editing a text is much like the psychoanalytic process. Textual analysis is the exploration of the
product of another's mind, including unconscious influences on
the text. In editing as in psychoanalysis, a lot of personal information is revealed to a figure of transferred familial power. Being
intimately exposed to someone who will take on the task of discerning the author's intentions and making sure she is true to
them is not only similar to psychoanalysis, it has the same
implicit potential for intense psychological confrontation.

The difference is that the profound transference between
author and editor, very much the twin of the psychoanalytic
transference, is unacknowledged as such. Furthermore, this
potentially explosive confrontation takes place in a completely
unclinical environment with few restraints on the transference
phenomenon. Evidence of these relationships are mutely
attested to in the epigraphs of books where authors sometimes
deify their editors. Conversely, with a negative transference,
authors may bad-mouth their editors at literary receptions and
cocktail parties.

PARANOIA AND ART

---

*S*UPERFICIALLY, paranoia bears some resemblance to the creative process. In both cases a rich, new world is constructed. In reality the two systems are incommensurable. Unlike a paranoid system, with all its hidden reference and codified representations, a work of art often includes unresolvable references, which, like music, can only be articulated in terms of the work itself and do not refer to any symbolic system of reference outside of the work. For this reason paranoids, when faced with artistic productions, do not function critically at all. They fill anything they see with delusions of reference that have little relation to the work's intentions. In fact, paranoids have a very low tolerance for any initiative unmotivated by symbolism. Spontaneous improvisation, purely for its own sake, is absolutely beyond them. This accounts for the rigid austerity of their own productions when they operate within an artistic context. They cannot comprehend any artistic gesture that claims to have no function other than its appropriateness to the work.

As well, little is original in paranoid excess. The rationalizations and inverted cosmologies of a paranoid only appear rich and inventive. At a deeper level they are curiously stereotypical, they are flat and lacking insight. On the other hand, paranoiac systems bear a direct resemblance to critical and academic techniques of artistic interpretation. The critical method, by operation, must be somewhat paranoid. When faced with a new work of art, the critic has to presume as many intentionalities and hidden references as possible before selecting those that the artist most likely intended. The act of conjuring these potentialities, even if they are eventually rejected by the critic, parallels a para-noiac system. Salvador Dali intuited this in 1929 when he pro-posed his "paranoiac critical method."

A TEXT SHOUL D INCLUDE IT S OWN DECO DING INSTRU CTIONS

ARTISTIC INTEGRITY
AND THE CRITIC

A LL ARTISTS, particularly in the plastic arts, have an optimal progression for their work, a natural path. Under the
unforgiving discipline that total freedom imposes on the artist
(anything is possible, the only limit is the artist's imagination)
the question of integrity, of maintaining an uncompromised
progression of works that are each other's true siblings, is phe-
nomenally difficult. The task is made even harder in that the
series cannot be governed by conscious intention. It is impossible to second-guess oneself.

Because art creates its own context, the prerogative of the
critic is to examine the internal relations of an individual artist's
work within the aegis of the works' own hermeneutics. This
does not simply mean discerning the intentions and formal
necessities of the work's particular trajectory, but evoking the
language necessary to describe it. When this code has been bro-
ken, it is the critic's task to adjudicate the integrity of a given
work or series of works in terms of the artist's natural path.

Within the absolute freedom of such a self-created system
the critic must determine whether the artist has maintained the
discipline of "necessary forms." Has the artist enacted all available options in the search for the form of highest energy, the
nexus of signs which are the primary symbols within this particular artist's realm? Is the work truly original?

The critic's difficulty lies in differentiating the vital imperative that produces a natural series from a mere enactment of
options. It is possible, looking at the continuous elaboration of
forms provided by an artist, to see an inappropriate development, where the artist deviates from her innate path and suc-

cumbs to influences not proper to the development of her work. In a sense, determination of veracity is what critical acumen is all about. The critic must be able to perceive whether the artist is faithfully seeking the necessary next form, the actual subsequent step.

THE NATURAL PATH
OF THE ARTIST

*A*T THE BEGINNING of their career artists undertake a focusing procedure, which continues until they discover their innate mode of expression. In literature this is called "finding your voice." Artists can start the search for their voice at an almost arbitrary point, following the branching series of connections that is the path to their path. These connections are a related series of ideas, concepts and techniques linked by the artist's interest and curiosity, as well as by the necessities of the work at hand.

Eventually their path leads them to their "real" work—whatever it was that was in them to express. The branching series of connections that got them there then becomes the engine of their subsequent work. From this point it is simply a matter of maintaining their alignment with the true elaboration of forms intrinsic to them.

The success of this alignment is perceivable by both the artist and the outside observer, but only in retrospect. Each successive form in the sequence cannot be anticipated, neither by the artist nor by the critic.

PROFUNDITY

*P*ROFUNDITY is the temporal aspect of intelligence apparent only some time after exposure to a work of mind. It is
on a longer wavelength and cannot be grasped by either its creator or observer until it has manifested temporally. Even if spontaneous or improvisational intelligence (the shorter wavelengths
of intelligence) seems to be lacking in an individual, that individual's work can still manifest profundity over a period of time.
Profundity is like an invisible script that becomes legible only
through age.

WRITING

---

*L*ANGUAGE is an artificial intelligence, a self-perpetuating system in which we are all implicated and around which we cannot reason by any trick of speed. If something can be formulated in writing, then improvisational speed and spontaneous intelligence count for less when compared to the natural elaboration of a written train of thought. That is to say, writing duplicates the stylistic nature of profundity because of a parallel with its own strategy of self-perpetuation.

SHADOWS
OF THOUGHT

---

*W*ords are the shadows of thought. By ordering them within the full depth of their connotative charge, you obtain a mirror of thought. This sleight-of-hand (similar to the tricks that representational painters use to create an appearance of detail) creates a sequence of virtual thoughts.

In poetry, the ability of the poem to evoke meanings seemingly beyond the linguistic capability of its component words represents a transcendence of intention, the driving of consciousness through the conceptual perimeter of language.

Poems are the recombinant interplay of the shadows of ideas.

THE MUSES

*T*HE MUSE is a metaphor for the delegation of unconscious linguistic tasks. Of the nine muses, I am familiar with two—one for conversation and one for poetry. Both are purely vocabularistic, the central mechanisms to which we delegate the complexities of word choice and synonym-scanning in our memories. This is why the muses are called the daughters of memory, why they are personified as those agents that unconsciously scan memory for appropriate terms.

The muses are idiots savants, stand-ins for our own capacities, our personal linguistic abilities. They have to be regarded as outside forces because we cannot identify them with our personal will. They must remain unknowable because to take control of their functions would be as disruptive as trying to take over any other involuntary, subconscious function. The executive capability of consciousness, particularly in the realm of spontaneous improvisation, cannot, must not, know the workings of its parts.

LITERARY STYLE

*L*ITERARY STYLE is not intelligent in and of itself, though it can perform intelligently. This ability to simulate intelligence parallels the results obtained by aleatoric literary compositions such as William Burroughs's cut-ups, where meaning is generated through unexpected combinations of words and ideas. Moreover, the cycles and themes of a personal literary style can be comforting in that they establish a tactile narrative identity, which is an antidote to the pure, technical indifference of language.

Personal style is a sleight-of-hand because it creates an illusion of textural richness. The reader confuses stylistic uniqueness with information. The impression of richness is paradoxical considering how the repetition of personally standardized phrase types and syntactical rhythms represents a tendency towards homogeneity and therefore entropy. The super-imposition of these devices over a text that, if it were merely referential in a utilitarian sense, would be uninteresting, is not unlike a moiré pattern, where a coarse pattern is generated by the visual conflation of two finer patterns.

COMPOSITIONAL
STYLE AS
PATHOLOGY

---

*V*OCABULAR STYLE is the trace of personal choice in the field of synonymic contenders. Prose style consists of syntactical patterns that are grammatically conventional but stylistically original. There are important aspects of prose composition, however, that have no conventions. A few of these aspects include the introduction of new subjects, the sequence of points made (in expository prose) and the ordering of ideas and scenes in a text. By what authority, by what convention of rhetoric, in what manual of style do prose writers find how to order these components of discursive prose? How do they decide precisely where a particular textual development will occur, or where a commentary will be introduced into the subject under consideration? Why at one point and not another?

In any discursive writing what is being written is nothing but a series of outrageous, unfounded declarations. Examples, anecdotes and observations are brought in haphazardly, in a totally provisional structure. All we have as a guide, as a source of order, are prior texts and conventions. These conventions of style are just foils or simulations of personal strategies, which are themselves strategies of presentation and ordering, symptoms of hubris before the ultimate anarchy of any claim to special knowledge or even of something to say. It is all so arbitrary that stylistic mannerisms amount to a kind of pathology.

Pathetic paradigms of bankrupt notions of order.

SPEECH
MANNERISMS
AND LITERARY STYLE

$\mathcal{S}$tyle is a speech pathology you can work with as long as it isn't too chronic. It resides in the persistence of seemingly unconscious mannerisms that can be characterized as "pathological" in so far as they are repetitive and not under conscious control. An identifiable style is a personal location, like the call-sign for a radio station, which provides narrative continuity for the anxious reader who is ever in need of reassurance and confirmation of the author's identity.

Style is a logo. It represents an author's deviation from standard conventions of reference and becomes itself a signifying system, another layer of reference in addition to the standard nomination. This is similar to the manner in which the hostages of terrorists can convey secret messages to their relatives or countrymen simply through the mechanism of cultural familiarity. Using subtle variations from normal behaviour they can relate information that is culturally invisible to their captors.

Artists could be said to be hostages of their culture. By producing a stylistic system they create a counter-language subversive to the larger one.

COEVAL POETICS

*T*HE MOVEMENT of abstraction in poetry has generally, and by default, been towards the privatization of the image. Language-centred texts tend to be composed of a series of decontextualized images that are highly synopsized versions of larger, personal texts. They are secondary symbols combining referents idiosyncratic to the writer with those peculiar to the structure of individual poems (as well as those of general usage).

The de-privatization of the image in language-centred texts, a transcendence of self-reference, has paradoxically enhanced the privacy of this verse along with all the attendant implications of privilege entailed by that privacy. Even though the activities of language-centred writers have raised the stakes of abstraction, the end is unclear. Because language is self-referential, defining itself in terms of itself, there is a perimeter of reference outside of which the rules don't apply. To exceed this perimeter, regardless of the methodology used, is to arrive at a place where representation, and therefore words, fail, like internal combustion engines in the vacuum of space.

The excitement and joy in the best of coeval poetry is in the velocity at which the poet breeches the perimeter of reference and in the method or methods she uses. However, to prolong the trajectory beyond that perimeter, without constantly recharging the anti-referential engines within the confines of general usage, is to dissipate into an uncharted zone where maps are useless and the reader's investment dwindles to nothing.

SEMANTIC
DISPLACEMENT
IN THE POEM

---

*T*HE PERCEIVED READING of a word in a poem is often skewed as far as the intended meaning of the term is concerned. This is why a direct reference to the subject of the poem within the poem is almost always wrong. The consistency of this displacement is similar to that encountered by someone trying to spear a target underwater. The perceived location of an underwater object is always different from its actual location due to the diffractional bending of light by water. In both cases, the target and the poem, the displacement must be compensated for.

THE POEM'S
MISSING MASS

$\mathcal{E}$VEN the most representational poetry contains accessory meanings, which are unwritten. This paragrammatic material is the poem's "missing mass." The term "missing mass" is derived from astrophysics where it refers to the discrepancy between the theoretical mass of the universe and what is actually observed.

The poem is a field structure configured as much by its invisible parts as by its visible ones. The missing mass of the poem is a function of the semantic distance between the text and the reader.

A poem is like an isolated planet that has to create its own gravity in order to hold itself together. The poem's missing mass, which gives it thematic size, is like an artificial gravity. It generates the field structure of the poem and provides the poem with its unitary identity.

Poems are unitary constructs equal to themselves in all their parts. They are like instruments that cannot be played, or, when played, cannot be heard.

THE POEM AS
AN ARTIFICIAL
INTELLIGENCE

THE POEM'S business is to be of several minds, to contain evocative metaphors that, because new metaphors restructure reality, interact both with themselves and with the reader to create a new world. Due to the multiplicity of possible readings, the plurality of its connotative layers, the poem resonates with a paragrammatic ability to alter itself. It becomes a recursive, stacked, heuristic matrix. This matrix is like a separate intelligence, a node of artificial sentience. It is symbolically encoded in a language wrested from its own monstrous life. It is as if the poem waits to be decoded by a reader who can provide it with a surrogate heart.

Like film or music, poetry is a time-based art. The poem is an intruder alarm system wired to deliver pleasure. The reader, by bringing his or her semantic conditioning into a dislocative metaphorical field, trips a series of interpretive switches, and the whole poem's structure comes alive.

ETYMOLOGY
AND POETRY

THREE DISTINCT VECTORS intersect in the poem. The etymologically driven, diachronic subtext; the personal, idiosyncratic association-pattern of the individual poet; and the reader's imposition of conventional meaning. That is to say, the energy of the poem comes from the differential of intention between the momentum of a given word's etymological heritage, the expectations of narrative reference that we "read" into a given text, and the reader's anticipation of conventional meaning to create fresh meanings out of the unexpected juxtaposition of terms. Like atomic particles colliding in a cyclotron these linguistic juxtapositions reveal new, charmed constituents of meaning. Intention is harnessed, using its own protean energy to thrust into beauty.

GETTING IT WRONG:
THE ORIGIN OF
POETRY IN PARAPRAXIS

MISINTERPRETED METAPHORS, concepts and terms can be more useful than their original meanings. Mistakes (parapraxes) made while transcribing a poem are often more interesting than the original term and lead to a new version of a poem. It is as if mistakes were "holes" in the ostensible or "false" text, which the poet thinks she is working on, but which is, in actuality, only a superficial scrim hiding the real poem that lies behind the false one. If these "holes" are enlarged they will allow the real poem to emerge, birthed through the breech opened by the original mistake.

Some of the best poems have a quality of parapraxis to them, as though they were extricated slowly and with great labour from a mass of unintentional slips and "mistakes." These random elements can be reincorporated into the structure of the poem in a sort of reverse psychoanalysis where, instead of becoming explanations or interpretations of previously unconscious items, the unconscious material is projected into the real world in the corpus of the poem. Thus the poem becomes a formal conciliation between the structure of the poem and its content, the primordial forces of creation at the origin of the poem.

SHADOWS
OF
THOUGHT

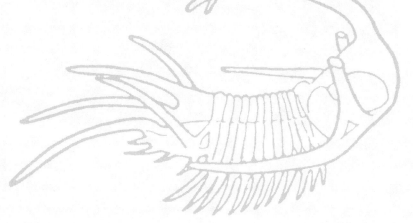

LANGUAGE

---

*C*O-ORDINATION of a nervous system that contains ten (to the eleventh power) neurons in the brain alone requires a high-level, integrative mechanism. Consciousness is this mechanism. Consciousness is a direct result of neural complexity. At some point on the road from *Homo erectus* to *Homo sapiens* the neuronal density of the cortex reached critical mass, and human consciousness was achieved. Communication between members of a species that has attained this consciousness requires a complex system of reference. Language is such a system.

Language is our collective project as a species. As in other cumulative undertakings of our species, such as the selective hybridization of domestic animals, its ontogeny exceeds the life span of the individual. No one person is responsible for coining the word *this*. However, language has had a much more profound effect on its creators than has the hybridization of domestic animals. In some respects, language can be conceived of as a self-replicating, lexical organism imbedded in our species. Its evolution, though inextricably bound to the biology of our own evolution, seems to have a synthetic life of its own. It isn't difficult to reverse the figure-ground relationship between humans and language, seeing language as an independent intelligence using humans as neural components in a vast and inconceivable sentience.

FITTING THE
LANGUAGE PROSTHESIS

---

*W*HEN we are born our brains are largely hard-wired. The visual cortex is "programmed" to see, and our motor cortex can already direct purposeful movements. Other parts of the brain are not hard-wired, however. Primary among these is the future speech centre. The speech centre is imprinted through acquisition of whichever language we are born into.

As we acquire a language our speech centres are rewired by that language. Through lack of use, redundant neural pathways atrophy so that the speech centres become imprinted with the abstract circuitry of language. The brain is physically remodelled by language.

Furthermore, the physical localization of certain functions, such as musical ability, are affected by our first language. Language acquisition is the beach-head of a process that eventually affects the whole of our consciousness.

Language can be regarded as a living software that has genetically earmarked a section of our brains for its own accommodation.

LANGUAGE
ACQUISITION TRAUMA

---

*A*T THE HEART of our experience of language lie the scars and trauma of some of our earliest frustrations and humiliations. From infancy our individuality is subsumed by consensually imposed meaning. What's more, we have to learn to express our most primal fears and desires using an abstract system of spoken symbols.

As infants we are fitted with a cognitive prosthesis, in much the same way that wild horses are forced to wear bits, braces and saddles. We come to realize that the adults in our lives (already perceived as omniscient, willful and possessing great knowledge) are hopelessly advanced in a system of communication that uses a secret verbal code. Only slowly do we master this system, and regardless of how much encouragement we receive from adults we continue to doubt that we will ever attain their level of sophistication.

Not surprisingly then, the central component of language acquisition trauma is performance anxiety, an anxiety we never fully put behind us.

REFERENCE
AND REALITY

---

*M*OST of our learning is mediated through the agency of language, an abstract, self-referential system of significa-tion. After the first few verbal acquisitions of childhood the majority of our descriptive/linguistic terms are derived from other two-dimensional signs. The world is revealed to us by rela-tions of signs. Even as adults we rarely encounter anything we haven't already learned by its nominative description. Moreover, we habitually deal with representations of representations. We call the depiction of something (either a drawing or photo-graph) by the name of the object depicted. Although education claims to have informed us about the external world, we can only claim with any certainty that what we have actually acquired is the ability to manipulate a system of signifiers.

That is why, when we see the names of things associated with their objects, for instance when on nature trails the names of trees are affixed to their trunks, it may strike us as funny. It's the same humour that Magritte played upon when he called his painting of a pipe "Ceci n'est pas une pipe." There is something inherently paradoxical about juxtaposing a name and its object in a three-dimensional continuum, although, in reality, this is only the external demonstration of an internal process we habit-ually use and rarely question.

Personal pronouns are the only instances where this discrep-ancy doesn't apply. They are so intimately associated with their objects that badges and name tags do not elicit the same reac-tions as labels on nature trails.

NAMES

$\mathcal{P}$ERSONAL PRONOUNS have the least amount of grammatical meaning of any term in our language. They are more like labels or indexes with a single use. Our name is a prosthesis we adapt to, grow to identify with. Our personal pronoun is a handle by which we can be manipulated as an abstract unit within the larger operations of language.

LANGUAGE IS A COGNITIVE PROSTHESIS

REPRESENTATION
AND CONTROL:
NOMINATIVE
AUTHORITY

*N*AMING is an absolution of the crisis of identification, the antidote to visual agnosia. Naming is proof of knowledge, and through that knowledge, of mastery. It indicates first-hand experience on behalf of the user.

When children acquire names from adults, when the child says, "What's that?" the term the adult gives the object both represents and confers the experience and knowledge of the adult to the child. The adult's familiarity with an object is transferred by the adult's nominative authority of the term, even if the named object remains a mystery for the child in terms of its function and relation to other objects. The child presupposes that the adult possesses a much more profound knowledge of the world than the adult actually does. This is a learned response, for not only does the name not "explain" the object, it complicates it by introducing a linguistic association. However, none of this interferes with the process of magical transference by which the naming of an object allays the enigma of identity for the child.

IDIOSYNCRATIC
LEXICONS

---

*A*LL OF US carry around idiosyncratic definitions of words that arise from unique, personal precedents and juvenile misinterpretations. The emotional and physical context of our first encounter and use of a particular word colours and defines it for us, "sets" its meaning. Within general usage there is a high degree of subjective variability.

LANGUAGE I
S PURE AUTO
SUGGESTION

ETYMOLOGY

$\mathcal{E}$VERY WORD has its own genealogy of meaning, its own hoard of historical connotations. This etymology is the subconscious text, the meaning under the level of conversation. It is the source of some of the associative moods that flavour and inform both conversation and text, an unconscious influence derived from ancestral connotations. Conceivably, this hidden etymology could be made explicit by a phatic reading of the words, voicing their primitive, subtextual meanings. Etymology is a vast, interlocking network of discourse behind discourse.

WORDS AS ADAPTERS

---

*D*EVICES that allow dissimilar pieces of equipment to be connected are called adapters. Because words possess an idiosyncratic, personal interpretation as well as their public, consensual meanings, they are, in effect, universal adapters. The consensual, general meaning of words permits discrepancies between the personal vocabularies of conversationalists to be transcended. This allows two dissimilar people to communicate.

However, because a consensual definition is a limiting constraint on meaning, proscribing personal valences, it follows that all words are generalizations that enact a theft of meaning. In conversation this theft of meaning takes place not only on the verbal level but also on the conceptual plane, especially if you succeed in imposing a particular definition on your conversational partner either by complicit agreement or by argument. Because your partner must realign his or her reality to understand what you are saying, every "understanding" is a loss.

WORDS

1.1   Words are stencils.

1.11   We understand by the outline of words.

1.12   Words have no substance.

1.3   They are an absence through which we frame their ostensible objects.

1.32   A frame is a characterization.

SYNTAX

1.1　Syntax is the stylistic equivalent of individuality.

1.2　The individual is an idiosyncratically associative mode enacting its personal world model.

1.21　The world model is itself recursively engendered by the associative domain of language.

1.3　Syntax is the thread of alignment along which meaning condenses.

2.0　Syntax is creation anticipated.

3.0　Reference/signification is memory.

3.1　Without memory, movement is impossible.

4.0　Reverence in the deferential treatment of ideation by the signifiers

SYNONYMIC REDUNDANCY AND TELEOTROPISM IN SENTENCES

*L*ANGUAGE is always movement forward, streamlined into the anticipation of an ultimate meaning. Meaning is where we are going, it is our intention. Like a plant growing towards light, a sentence grows towards its final meaning, it is teleotropic. This ultimate meaning is the orientation of a sentence at any given point in time. It is a magnetic field in which syntax is the compass needle pointing to the true north of intention.

Both speech and writing are anticipatory motions, propelled by the expectation of sense. The burden of teleotropism, of intention, creates a performance anxiety deep at the root of our apparent linguistic facility. The continual flight of the point of concentration, tracking within the superstructure of intention as a nomadic moment of attention, makes for a restless, anxious lack of stasis.

Like music, discursive language creates self-relational structures whose meaning depends on particular successions of elements. This is both the impatience and the sensuality of the text. Also, because discourse is a time-dependent activity, like improvised music, the exigencies of its production provide a limited temporal window for individual components (words) in the construction of its spontaneous sequences. At the speed of normal conversation there is not a lot of time to vacillate over choices of terms.

Recourse to synonymic alternatives ensures the forward momentum of discourse. These redundancies, which have been built in to language, make sure that the speed of communication is unhampered by laborious, time-wasting searches for appropriate terms. They are margins of allowance, like back-up systems, ensuring that a connection be there when you need it.

Whatever gets you there.

THE BREACH OF INTENTION IN THE NARRATIVE ECONOMY OF TIME

*T*HE IMPROVISATIONAL SPEED of discourse enforces a strict adherence to rapid choices. Language is a full-speed-ahead situation. Even a vague connection, a provisional linguistic sketch, must instantly take the full weight of intention by conforming to the expectations of meaning in a given sentence's momentum. This is why a speaker who has not quite decided between two similar terms such as "shout" and "cheer" will combine them in an inadvertent neologism, in this case, "chout." In a militaristic analogy you could say that intention, the ultimate meaning of a sentence, is like an army that must pass through the narrow passage of each successive term that supports it. In other words, the whole army of metaphors, clauses, subjects and verbs are committed at any given moment to one breach in the beach-head of incomprehension. Every term is the breach of intention, sacrificing itself in reference for the higher aim of communication.

The interchangeability of terms is the local manifestation of a language characteristic that exists on a global scale as well, translating languages being merely a scaled-up version of synonymic redundancy. It is important to remember that the source of this substitutional arbitrariness—the linguistic symbol—is not arbitrary due to the inherent symbolic nature of abstract thought itself. It is arbitrary out of pure practicality, so that other terms can take its place in the dynamic circumstances of conversation.

WIND-ROSES, ETYMOLOGICAL TUNNELS AND THE PARADIGMATIC AXIS

---

*W*E ARE generally unaware of how the deep structure of language directs and controls communication. In fact the software of language alters the nature of our consciousness. As infants it gives us the metaphorical armature from which we derive our general conceptualizations. The layered complexity of language consists of its etymological and emotional derivations, as well as the interlinked associative matrices that drive conversation.

In his book *Course in General Linguistics*, Ferdinand de Saussure outlined two aspects of language, which he characterized spatially. One he named the *syntagmatic*. This referred to the horizontal, linear relation between words in a sentence and the grammatical interdependence of terms in a given communication. It was always directed towards a cumulative discharge of meaning at the completion of a sequence. The other term he introduced was the *paradigmatic*, which described a vertical array of synonyms and personal associations intersecting the syntagmatic axis at a right angle, above and below each word in a sentence. This vertical inventory of alternatives makes communication easier due to the availability of equivalent terms. According to Robert Scholes: "Our actual selection of a word in a sentence involves something like a rapid scanning of paradigmatic possibilities until we find the one that will play the appropriate role in the syntax we are creating."

By taking the example word "lightning" and arranging the associative and synonymous terms above and below it we can produce a diagram of paradigmatic relations. Proximity in this arrangement indicates a particular term's appropriateness relative to the semantic intention of the sentence in which "lightning" occurs.

park

flash

electricity

Lightning

shock

fire

charge

By diagramming an example sentence in this manner we can see some interesting relations between surface and deep associational structure in the fabric of everyday discourse.

any	branch	recently	blasted	from	spark
that	bush	been	hammered	for	flash
a	shrub	were	hit	with	electricity
The	**tree**	**was**	**struck**	**by**	**lightning.**
an	foliage	had	jolted	through	shock
this	plant	have	slammed	to	fire
our	vegetation	past	assailed	as	charge

Notice that we can thread together any linear combination of synonymous terms, choosing paths at random, and still maintain nearly all of the narrative information of the original sentence. For example: "That bush were jolted with electricity," or even "Our foliage been hit by spark." Notice also the cluster of metaphoric terms around the verb and its synonyms.

Elaborating on this model we can illustrate the temporal function of the syntagmatic axis by replacing the paradigmatic axis with a representation of the accumulation of intended meaning in a given communication. In a sense a sentence has a negative semantic value (in relation to its total meaning) until its given content or message has been achieved. Each sequential increment of information marks a fraction of the final whole. Subjects and verbs, which contain the bulk of the content of a sentence, will accordingly have higher completion levels compared to words whose functions are more purely grammatical. A diagram depicting the syntagmatic or temporal function of discourse might resemble the following:

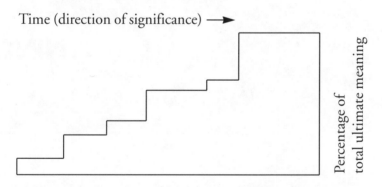

Time (direction of significance) ⟶

Percentage of total ultimate meaning

The tree was struck by lightning.

The level of expectation of meaning in a given sentence is directly proportional to its length. This expectation of meaning, the graphic curiosity that fuels the engine of reading, will look for meaning even when there is none. In fact, in the total absence of meaning, such as a random string of words, the reader will use this expectation to fabricate meaning out of chaos. Mood and personal association patterns become the two main operators of a given reader's interpretation of obscure or ambiguous communication.

In order to integrate the information from the paradigmatic and the syntagmatic/temporal axes, you need a third axis. By using a lateral dimension you can effectively show the relationship between the paradigmatic and syntagmatic qualities of discourse. The paradigmatic arrays are represented as circular. In this model the appropriate term is at the centre of the "target" disc of synonyms, with less synonymous terms relegated to a periphery that, hypothetically, is contingent with, or bleeds synonymically, into the rest of the terms in a personal lexicon. For clarity's sake this indistinct border zone at the margin of the paradigmatic disc is not represented.

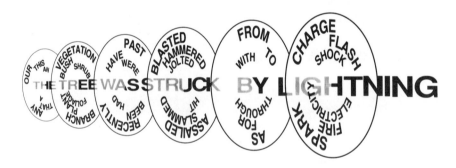

Paradigmatic Discs

Each disc also represents the present moment of the individual, the now of consciousness informed by the personal, associational word hoard. The paradigmatic disc is a snapshot of a single flux pattern excerpted from the totality of personal flux patterns. Inherent in this momentary focus are the historical experiences that make up the individual as these are brought to bear on the moment. Memory is active throughout the length of the sentence. Each prior disc influences its successor by leaving traces of itself in memory; after-images, which are navigational aids maintaining syntagmatic direction. It could be said that the progress of the disc through a given string of words, a sentence, a communication, leaves a semantic trail, a record of its passage, incorporating both the emotional and informative events of its transit through the syntagmatic axis. The contours of this passage constitute a texture, a tactile synthesis of the boundary of self and text.

The syntagmatic axis is the axis of memory. The sentence has a local, syntagmatic memory, proper to its functioning, as well as a historical memory, the diachronic origin of its terms. This historical, etymological axis, although in a metaphoric sense simply an extension in magnitude of syntagmatic memory, can be regarded as an addition to the three axes of functional discourse. It is a fourth axis that parallels the syntagmatic axis. Each word in a sentence brings with it its own etymological history. Visualized, it would be a tunnel whose walls undergo gradual transformations through the evolution of a term. There are points within a word's derivation where it can have meanings quite dissimilar to its contemporary usage. A term comes to us with all its history intact, though these derivations operate on a subconscious level within the sentence. It is as if a word's etymological character, a quality of its overall meaning, were an indispensable component of its connotative viability. This diachronic connotation evokes the deep symbolism of a word and is often synchronous with the emotional subtext of a given communication.

In the following diagram, two words are shown in front of their respective etymological tunnels. Each term is traced back to its Old Norse form, such that *went* regresses through *wendan* and *venda* to arrive at the Old Norse term *wandjan*, and *on* returns through *an* and *aan* to arrive at *ā*.

Synchronic View of Etymological Tunnels

To incorporate this fourth axis into the diagram of the syntagmatic axis threading the paradigmatic discs would overly complicate it. By manipulating your visualization of the paradigmatic discs, rotating them until you view them edge on (if they do, indeed, have edges), you can project the semantic components out of each side. Not only can you display another level of complexity and still maintain a degree of simplicity within the illustration but you can also demonstrate the symmetry of a complementary relation between the two paradigmatic arrays.

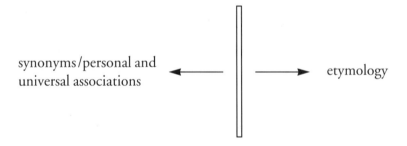

synonyms/personal and universal associations ←——— ———→ etymology

Side View of Paradigmatic Disk

If you drop the purely synonymous terms from this associative category, the display can be developed into an even more symmetrical elaboration by following the formal correspondences between these two refined axes through successively deeper semantic levels of discourse, as in the following diagram:

Personal Associations	Etymology
Personal history of individual. Ontogenesis. Individuality. Psyche.	History of language. Diachronic evolution. Collective, archetype.
Synchronic/paradigmatic subtext is what the individual brings to a word.	Diachronic/etymological subtext is what language (as a collective project) brings to the word.

In so far as we are formed by the language, there is, naturally, a high degree of correlation between a word's personal associations and its etymological derivation. If you use the word *window* as an example you can easily see the correspondence. Window can be traced back to the Middle English form *windoge* and from there to the Old Norse term *vind-auga* or wind eye. *Wind* derives from the Old Norse *vindr*, originally present participle of the Aryan verb in German *wehen*, weather. *Eye* returns through the Anglo-Saxon *eage* and the Old Norse *auga* back to the Sanskrit *akshi*. The Lower German form, *oegeln*, to look at, itself derived from *oege*, eye, survives today in the term *ogle*. Any personal associative derivation of "window" will probably encounter one complex of associations that devolve on weather and the idea of looking at, or regarding, the weather.

For example, we could free-associate starting from the immediate and concrete perception of a window, which is the experience of glass and transparency, through the relational concepts of interiority/exteriority, into the personal experiential associations from memory-specific occasions of observing the weather, the seasons and the alternation of night and day into the seasons and the passage of time. From there we could move into still more personal associations—the pale reflection of one's face superimposed over the landscape behind the window. This dichotomous though complementary relationship is shown in the following diagram, where the gradient of the personal moves upwards from the universal.

reflections
weather/seasons/time
interiority/exteriority
observation
glass

Window

Middle English: wind-oge
Old Norse:　　　vind-auga (wind eye)

At this point you can resurrect the synonymous terms, lost during the manipulation of our transcended model, by adding a third axis to the new model. We now have an "exploded" view of an individual word's components, which includes the whole of its paradigmatic field, both the personal associations and the synonyms of common usage, as well as the diachronic information contained in the etymology, in a sort of meta-syntagmatic axis. The only axis not represented in the following diagram is the syntagmatic axis of the sentence from which "window" was taken.

aperture
porthole
opening

Window

Middle English: wind-oge
Old Norse:　　　vind-auga (wind eye)

reflections weather/seasons/time interiority/exteriority observation glass

Marine navigation charts use a symbol called a wind-rose. This symbol consists of a circular array of feathered shafts of various lengths, which represent the average percentages of time that a wind blows from a particular point of the compass as well as the average force of that wind. Several wind-roses dotted over a nautical map look not unlike feathery, geometric snowflakes. If you imagine the sentence to lie flat, on a plane, as indeed it does on a page, then by extending this plane you can derive a surface equivalent to the surface of an ocean. The entailment of this planar metaphor would liken the invisible forces of the wind to the unseen and silent paradigmatic forces that influence the visible/audible discourse.

Using as an example the sentence "Outside her cabin window the ocean was grey and angry," you can calibrate fairly precisely the exact nuances of connotation in a highly diagrammatic manner for the chosen term *window*. Using a paradigmatic wind-rose consisting of an abbreviated usage-specific paradigmatic array, you can measure the force and direction of the connotative winds of nuance as they blow over the surface of the text. You can calibrate the exact drift of intention from the projected course of the discourse.

porthole

weather **Window**

Old Norse-vind-auga

This is a relatively innocuous example with little semantic freight other than its descriptive function in a prose narrative. The paradigmatic wind-roses of the associatively laden terms found in literature, particularly poetry, have much more convoluted and idiosyncratic derivations.

CONSCIOUSNESS
AS METAPHORICAL

---

*W*E INTERPRET present phenomena in the light of past experience. Regardless of the predictive efficacy of this technique we are "understanding one thing in terms of another," as George Lakoff defines metaphors. We use the past as metaphor to apprehend the present. Our cognitive processes, our thoughts and consciousness, are based entirely on metaphor.

A PERIODIC TABLE
OF THE TROPES

$\mathcal{A}$ CCORDING TO George Lakoff, professor of linguistics at the University of California in Berkeley, metaphor is ubiquitous in language and is not limited to figures of speech. He suggests, for example, that even simple prepositions such as *on, under* or *through*, by generalizing or characterizing spatial relations, act as low-grade metaphors. In this way it is easy to see how all of language is based on metaphor and on the shifting, elusive relations that metaphor engenders.

Metaphors are more than just figures of speech. They are cognitive devices we use to interact with the world. An apt metaphor allows us to manipulate information effectively, while an inapt metaphor can obscure the solution to important problems. Nowhere are metaphors more important than in economics and social sciences. Misrepresenting our economy with inappropriate metaphors can exacerbate a bad situation. For example, characterizing the economy as an engine during a recession, as in "Trying to kick-start the economy," may not be as effective as visualizing it as a journey: "We are on the road to recovery."

In the months prior to reading Lakoff I'd been attempting to classify the tropes, partially for my own elucidation and partially to find out if they had an order that would become obvious once I'd assembled them in one place. Certain natural groups were immediately apparent. Similes, for example, are merely qualified metaphors. Likewise, allegories and parables are extended narrative metaphors. Symbols and signs, on the other hand, eluded these natural categories. In one sense symbols are very close to metonyms; in another they are like signs. Signs are seemingly without cultural context (in that they are arbitrary, like braille, for example) and they are also totally substitutional.

It was while trying to place these more problematic members that I developed a strategy to facilitate the overall classification. This strategy is based on general properties inherent to all metaphors. It defines both their species, by natural grouping, and their position in the developmental hierarchy, that is to say, their position relative to a scale of increasing sophistication that appears to have originated in hyperbole and personification and, ultimately, to have led to metaphor and analogy.

Eventually I arranged the tropes in the following general families: SUBSTITUTIONAL (it can be argued that these are not even tropes, but they bear inclusion because, although they are not things understood in terms of other things, they are things standing for other things and as such have a direct relation to the tropes proper), which includes *signs*, *symbols* and the act of *signifying*; EXAGGERATIVE, which includes *hyperbole*; SYMPATHETIC, which includes *personification*; ASSOCIATIVE, which includes *synecdoche*, *metonymy* and *euphemisms*; COMPARATIVE, which includes *similes, metaphors, allegories, parables* and *analogies*; and finally the ULTRA-COMPARATIVE/SYNONYMOUS, which includes the mathematical concept of *isomorphism*. This last category, in its abstraction, is very close to the purely substitutional nature of the sign, on which all language is based and which gives language its highly abstract, synesthetic, cross-modal foundation. It seems appropriate that just as each end of the electromagnetic spectrum is invisible to the naked eye, so do the tropes graduate into abstraction at each end of their scale.

The definitions for the following terms have been derived and paraphrased from standard reference works.

The Periodic Table of the Tropes

Substitutional

Symbol   Something used for or regarded as representing something else. Something that stands for, represents or denotes something else, particularly a material object that represents something immaterial or abstract, as "•" represents a new moon.

Signify / Sign   To mean. To make known by signs, speech or action. To be a sign or symbol of, to represent. Letters signify sounds as words signify sound / meaning aggregates, as "4" represents four things.

Exaggerative

Hyperbole   Obvious and intentional exaggeration, an extravagent statement not intended to be taken literally, as in "to wait for an eternity."

Sympathetic

Personification   The attribution of human characteristics to something nonhuman, as in "the rocks shivered in the cold."

Associative

Metonym
A word used in a transferred sense. A figure of speech that consists of substituting for the name of a thing the name of one of its attributes or of something closely related. Reference by contiguity. The use of the name of one object or concept for that of another to which it is related, or of which it is a part, as "sceptre" represents sovereignty, or "the bottle" stands for strong drink.

Synecdoche
A figure by which the whole stands for the part or the part for the whole, or by which the special stands for the general or the general for the special, as "ten sails" represents ten ships or the "breaking of bread" represents eating a meal in company or a "roof over our heads" represents a house.

Euphemism
The substitution of a mild or vague expression for a harsh or blunt one, as in "ladies of the night" instead of prostitutes.

Comparative

Metaphor
The application of a word or phrase to an object or concept that it does not literally denote in order to suggest comparison with another object or concept, as in "the law is a fortress." The application of a descriptive term to an object to which it is not literally applicable, as in "a glaring error."

Simile	A figure of speech in which two unlike things are explicitly compared by the use of comparative conjunctions such as *like, as, so,* etc., as in "the lake is like glass," or "skin as soft as velvet."
Allegory	A story or narrative, as a fable, in which a moral principle or abstract truth is presented by means of fictional characters, events, etc. A representation of an abstract or spiritual meaning through concrete or material forms, or figurative treatments of one subject under the guise of another. "The Boy Who Cried Wolf" is an allegory.
Parable	A fictitious narrative used to illustrate a moral or spiritual principle such as "The Parable of the Talents" in the Bible.
Analogy	A partial similarity between like features of two things on which a comparison might be based, as the relation between pages of a book and "layers of limestone." Agreement or resemblance in certain aspects, as form or function, between otherwise dissimilar things. Similarity without identity.

Ultra-Comparative / Synonymous

Isomorphism	Mathematical. A term describing two groups that correspond to each other in form and in the nature and product of their operations. In Burnside's 1897 publication, *Group Theory*, it was set out as follows: "If a correspondence

can be established between the operations of G and G' so that to every operation of G there corresponds a single operation of G' while to the product A B of any two operations of G there corresponds the product A'B' of the two corresponding operations of G' then the groups G and G' are said to be simply isomorphic." (It could be argued that the magnetically aligned ferrous particles on the surface of audio tape stand in an isomorphic relation to the music they represent when they are drawn across the playback head of a cassette player.)

Imposing a hierarchic map on the tropes is a risky business. There are, however, some obvious developmental stages, particularly in the way that language and abstract reasoning is acquired by children. The relation between personification, hyperbole and metaphor is a case in point. It seems that personification is an intermediary developmental stage between literalness and metaphor. It also seems proper to place hyperbole anterior to personification because, although hyperbole verges on metaphor, it is not actually a comparison between two otherwise dissimilar things.

In children, personification is an early method of identification with objects (and their attendant manipulational functions). Play is a natural extension of this personification, which gradually facilitates the child's conceptual manipulation of abstract symbols through fantasies. Furthermore, personification habituates the child to the wider range of identities, strategies and empathies that are necessary adult skills. Personification transforms causal reality into personal, bite-sized chunks that the child can handle. Hyperbole, like personification, is prior to comparative metaphor because it maintains subject-continuity. Something is merely compared to an extreme version of itself.

Exaggeration, however, is the beginning of the plastic process of comparison, which ends in metaphor.

There are even more complications to this chart. For example, there is a movement within metonymy and synecdoche towards symbol through the process of diachronic detachment; that is, a tendency of figures of speech to evolve into pure signs whose only causal link with their original object is a single, historically distant antecedent. The phrase "throw in the towel" is such a term. Its original meaning, in the context of boxing, is lost, though its gist survives in the phrase. Clearly, metaphors, at least conventional metaphors, constantly evolve into signs, and in this abandonment of historical origins their previous associations evaporate. Perhaps *sign* should be at the top of the chart. Tribal icons and hieroglyphs contain synecdochic representations of the objects they represent and might also be historically prior to abstract systems of signification such as written language.

It could be argued that synecdoche has perceptual priority and is closer to the origin of metaphor than are the other tropes. The fact that we focus only on one feature of our environment at a time indicates that synecdoche is a paradigm of conscious attention. For example, we look at people's hands to see if they are tense or relaxed, and we refer to others by single features, such as "My brown-eyed girl." We are constantly interpreting the world through its particulars and deriving the general from the specific. Synecdoche has a direct, bio-perceptual basis.

Analogy, as well, is difficult to place within the metaphoric continuum. Because it is so similar to the concept of isomorphism it would seem appropriate to put it, as I have done, at the end of the chart. On the other hand it has a more primitive aspect than, say, a particularly apt metaphor and might be better placed anterior to metaphor proper. Also, euphemisms are merely inverted hyperboles. Instead of exaggerating their object in a hyperbolic manner euphemisms de-emphasize it. This leads right into the same classificational difficulties I had earlier. Is the tendency *towards* or *away from* sophistication? Should this chart include paradigms, ideals and prototypes?—they could be said to have a metonymous relation to the categories they represent. Perhaps, ultimately, all these classifications are spurious, being superseded by Lakoff's ubiquitous model where all of language seems fair game as metaphor, unconstrained to figures of speech.

What *is* certain is that on its micro-scale, in the realm of the sign, language is infinitely substitutional and arbitrary. On its macro-scale, at the level of intention and meaning, language is associative and comparative and aspires towards the isomorphic ideal of reference. Even though isomorphisms are not actually present in language, they nevertheless exert an ideal to which the comparative impulse tends. In the largest sense they are substitutional, like synonyms. Thus substitution—infinite, utilitarian and anonymous at one end, referential, finite and unique at the other—parenthesizes the metaphoric spectrum.

THE TRANSFORMATIVE
POWER OF DIALOGUE

---

*D*IALOGUE is the substrate of creativity and personal growth. All conversation is inevitably self-interrogation through the agency of another, who, by creating or providing discontinuities unavailable to one's habituated patterns of thought, provides new perspectives and insights, generating real innovation and true personal growth.

Conversations sometimes uncover pre-conscious or previously unarticulated ideas in one of the speakers. Like search planes, conversations can range widely, locating missing or unarticulated fields of thought that otherwise might have evaded consciousness. For this reason the interview is an exemplary vehicle for self-discovery.

Dialogue is the friction that polishes our minds.

CONCRETE
TECHNICAL
REALITY

LIFE

MOUNTAINS, NIETZSCHE
AND AERIAL LANDSCAPES

*N*ietzsche formulated much of his later philosophical work while hiking through the mountains near Sils Maria. The fabled subjectivism of his philosophy was mirrored in the alpine landscape he walked through. Mountain topography, with its epic scale, is nonetheless intimate and subjective because it has no horizon. There is no "beyond," only the multiplicity of vertical landscapes, a sheltering enclosure.

Elevated and inclined slopes are aerial landscapes. According to Barthes the aerial landscape is an intellectual landscape because we operate not in it but upon it, abstracted by an objective viewpoint equivalent to an exterior point of view. The territory is at once real and a map. Mountainous terrain creates a state of optical omniscience, which subtly conditions the person experiencing such a landscape to see material reality in larger, more generalized and abstracted portions.

The mind's eye, from the vantages offered in alpine elevations, can obviously comprehend geographical relationships on a much vaster scale than can an observer imbedded in that geography. At enough distance orogeny and erosion become self-evident. Even if you are not prone to thinking in generalizations, or abstractly in large orders of magnitude, the mountainous landscape induces a generalizing and aphoristic disposition in those who experience it. It perceptually reinforces the philosophical inclination to combine discrete portions of information into generalizations.

A true aphorism works both ways—its particularities must derive from the general.

MOUNTAIN SILENCE

*T*HERE IS an absorbent silence in the mountains, which becomes more intense towards their peaks. It imparts a curious aural quality to summit ambience, a preternatural stillness such that even the wind, rising up the windward side of the mountain, cannot completely break it. Even on the wildest days the stillness lurks in the mountain lee, a thick, velvet silence.

This quality of muffled "thickness" is an illusion, however, arising from the lack of background noise. At higher altitudes you are increasingly more alone, elevated from the ambient noise of planar existence. This is the source of mountain silence, the falling away of background noises, an absolute reduction of their sources.

SEEING THE WIND

---

*T*HE WIND is neither uniform nor constant. It is a turbulent concatenation of billows and vortices, of twisting strands and planar surfaces. It rolls into irregular cylinders and is at once quick and viscous, full of spirals and interwoven eddies. The shape of the wind can be seen in many things, in flags and smoke. Gusts can be watched as they traverse water, and zephyrs imprint their transient shapes in sheets hung out to dry on clotheslines. Kites calibrate gusts as they pass, and you can see waves of wind as they move through the crowns of distant trees.

WATER

WATER demonstrates itself, it is absolutely explicit. Water is transparent to both light and energy. In its liquid state it is almost a perpetual-motion machine, endlessly reflecting and re-reflecting any movement that has been impressed on it. Light and motion diminish only gradually in its interior. Because it is almost infinitely permeable to energy it has the ability to transmit conflicting energies as wave-fronts through itself. It can effortlessly conduct the backwash from an entire coastline through oncoming waves without losing any of the information in either of the opposing systems. Water is a uniform, self-consistent substance that can contain great complexities of energy and yet maintain lucid simplicity. It behaves in its parts as it does in its whole.

OBJECTS
ARE OCCASIONS

$\mathcal{E}$VERYTHING is an occasion. A rock is an event. All objects are events. A rock or a planet merely occupies a location and volume for a period of time. A human being is a mobile occasion.

THE BREAKDOWN
OF UNIQUENESS
IN THE MICROVERSE

*H*OMOMORPHISM, or likeness of form, is a fundamental characteristic of our universe. Galaxies are alike, as are spider monkeys, carbon atoms and Ford Fairlanes. At the opposite pole, uniqueness is equally ubiquitous in the universe. At every scale of matter, excluding the subatomic, no two things are absolutely alike.

With large-scale serial copies, such as humans and cars, difference is identity, uniqueness. Uniqueness could be said to be the most basic sort of information exchange. As long as both copies are conscious and able to detect their differences or, conversely, as long as there are conscious beings to determine the difference between copies, then information is exchanged.

Uniqueness, however, appears to break down at the quantum level. Subatomic particles such as electrons are completely identical. When two subatomic particles are close enough together, their identities merge into a region, their spatial uniqueness becomes indeterminate. Trying to imagine this absolute identicality is deeply counter-intuitive because it is fundamentally incomprehensible. Nothing in our experience prepares us for it.

It is as if the Platonic notion of ideal forms exists in physical reality at the subatomic level, where identity becomes generic. This absolute identicality simply *is*. It is an identicality that doesn't exist on any other plane of matter, although it could exist in the imagination. Perhaps in the quantum microverse, matter and energy are functions of the charge created by spatial separation. Perhaps the fact that matter exists at all is due to the energy derived from the creation of difference by spatial separation.

Nothingness is also identical to itself. If time and space are functions of each other, then the smallest spatial separation could set heaven and earth apart.

A singularity at the beginning of time.

TIME AND
RANDOMNESS

---

*A*T ANY GIVEN MOMENT, "moment" is solid. If time
could be stopped, the frozen universe would be entirely
deterministic. Everything in it would have an invariable and
absolute relation to every other thing. This idea is similar to
Leibniz's theory of retrospective determinism, which he outlined in his book *Discourse on Metaphysics.* In it he states that,
hypothetically, you could write a mathematical equation that
described any existing configuration of lines.

If a scientist had complete access to a hypothetical universe
where time had stopped and she then developed a system that
would predict, perfectly, the behaviour of every particle in that
universe when time recommenced, what would happen when
time actually did recommence? No matter how perfectly predictive her system was it could never, ultimately, forecast what
would happen in that universe for even a second after time had
started again. Time causes turbulence in deterministic systems;
it introduces randomness.

Random number generators are electronic devices used by
scientists to produce "random" numbers. The pure random,
however, is an unknowable, relational quality. In fact, because it
has not been absolutely quantified, it can be said that there are
no such things as random number generators given that they
work by mathematical principles that are themselves descrip-
tions (perhaps incomplete) of concepts of randomness. There
are only models of randomness. Perhaps the "random" exists
only as a mathematically privileged concept.

If this is the case, then the truly random may be our highest achievement, particularly if it somehow "exceeds" naturally occurring randomness.

TO EXPERIENC
E ETERNITY EV
EN FOR A SEC
OND IS TO EX
PERIENCE ALL
OF ETERNITY

TIME

---

*T*IME is the medium in which you go from one place to another.

SOFTWARE IS THE GHOST I N THE MACH INE

THE UNCANNY

---

*T*HE COINCIDENCE is a remarkable convergence of events. The uncanny is coincidence squared.

The uncanny event, which is an obvious singularity or convolution in the continuum, has a massive psychic gravity and affects personal models of reality immediately adjacent to it in much the same manner as a star bends light.

DEOXYRIBONUCLEIC
ACID

---

*N*EW SPECIES come from genetic mutations. Genetic mutations are caused by damage to DNA. This damage is a type of cosmic noise. Evolution proceeds through the natural selection of mutations. DNA is the selective interface between mutation and survival. Humans are the embodied memory of genetic evolution locked in one temporal direction by DNA.

LIFE UNITS

$\mathcal{A}$ LIFE UNIT can be described as any living thing containing replicative DNA. All life units are equal relative to the great dichotomy between animate and inanimate matter. Each life unit possesses a will. A will is tantamount to consciousness.

NATURE IS DI
VINE TECHN
OLOGY

INANIMATE   ANIMATE

organic molecules

minerals   clay   algae
                                    viruses
inert gases   enzymes
                                                insects
                                        amoebae
        chemical reactions

STATEMENT OF
FIRST PRINCIPLES

---

*H*UMANS are thinking animals. All animals are biological machines that perpetuate genes. Miracle is everywhere. That the universe has no creator is even more miraculous than if it did. Awe, wonder and religious grace are innate to the human psyche. Empirical reality can only enhance our spiritual nature.

Deistic explanations are a reduction of the singular amazingness of our world. They diminish reality by trivializing it, confusing it with mythology. Notions of an afterlife demean the sanctity and profundity of existence. Historically, belief in immortality has justified the slaughter of millions of human beings. Genocide incubates in the heart of monotheism.

The mind and brain are one. There is no immaterial soul distinct from the body. If you destroy part of the brain you also destroy part of what is called the soul. We intuitively assume that we possess an immaterial soul because our experience of consciousness is so smooth and continuous that we perceive it to be independent of its material basis. However, the biological conviction of our mortality and the absence of an afterlife is also intuitively, innately imbedded in our psyche. Deep down in every one of us is the frightening knowledge that the soul does not survive death. Part of our life task is to accept this mortality that is antithetical to the way that we experience ourselves.

Death is an illusion. "You" never die because you are not there to experience your being dead. Only those close to you experience the finality of your absence.

Everything we think, feel and see is materially based, a series of impulses and reactions within our brains. This does not "explain away" consciousness, it deepens the miracle. It is miraculous that we are finite, that we exist at all. It is even more miraculous and frightening that the entire universe is finite and appears to have arisen from a singularity in the midst of a timeless, spaceless continuum inconceivably less than nothing.